ALSO AVAILABLE FROM BLOOMSBURY

Death, Ritual, and Belief, Douglas J. Davies
9780304338221

Religion: Key Concepts in Philosophy, Brendan Sweetman
PB: 9780826486271
HB: 9780826486264

Myth: Key Concepts in Religion, Robert Ellwood
PB: 9781847062352
HB: 9781847062345

Ritual

Key concepts in religion

PAMELA J. STEWART
AND ANDREW STRATHERN

B L O O M S B U R Y

LONDON • NEW DELHI • NEW YORK • SYDNEY

Bloomsbury Academic

An imprint of Bloomsbury Publishing Plc

50 Bedford Square	1385 Broadway
London	New York
WC1B 3DP	NY 10018
UK	USA

www.bloomsbury.com

Bloomsbury is a registered trademark of Bloomsbury Publishing Plc

First published 2014

British Library Cataloguing-in-Publication Data
A catalogue record for this book is available from the British Library.

ISBN: HB: 978-1-44113-729-6
PB: 978-1-44118-569-3
ePub: 978-1-62356-846-7
ePDF: 978-1-62356-814-6

Library of Congress Cataloging-in-Publication Data
A catalog record for this book is available from the Library of Congress.

Typeset by Newgen Knowledge Works (P) Ltd., Chennai, India
Printed and bound in India

To the spirit in the giving

Pamela J. Stewart (Strathern) and Andrew J. Strathern
September 2012
Cromie Burn Research Unit

Contents

Preface

The topic of ritual has emerged recently as a major focus of academic interest. As a concept, the idea of ritual integrates the study of behavior both within and beyond the domain of religion. Ritual can be both secular and religious in character. There is renewed interest in questions such as: why do rituals exist at all? What has been, and continues to be, their place in society? How do they change over time? Such questions exist against a backdrop of assumptions about development, modernization and disenchantment of the world. The putative trajectories of historical change have become greatly more complex. Modernization as an ideology is set against postmodernism. The disenchanted world becomes influenced again by magical thinking, and rational political and economic theories scarcely seem to apply in a topsy-turvy of changes. Ritual appears then as a kind of constant that may help to afford a space for reflection, to slow down time, to restore order, or to assert, transform, and reassert identities. In this broad context, there is a place for a book which examines the field of ritual studies, looking at it both historically within anthropology and in terms of its contemporary relevance to phenomena such as healing rituals. Our overall analytical approach is that forms of ritual behavior and practice show commonalities across widely disparate geographical contexts; at the same time much can be learned from studying the special ways in which ritual activities connect with the broader social processes to which they belong. In other words, we look at commonalities across cultures, but we also look at specificities within cultural milieux. In pursuing this dual approach, we approach the general question 'why do rituals exist?' and also the specific questions of 'what is this ritual doing in its context here?'

Since interpretations of ritual have engaged the interests of social theorists for at least as long as the disciplines of sociology and anthropology have been practiced, we find it useful to organize our exposition partly along historical lines. We do this also because theories have changed over time. Some have become outmoded, others remain relevant today. Aspects of the old return in new guises. We will make these distinctions clear. Some definitional questions, however, need to be looked at first (see Chapter 1).

Ritual is such a broad topic, also, that any treatment of it has perforce to be selective. In our choice of materials here we have attempted to give some wide coverage of themes, expanding our account of some materials that are not so often looked at in depth and contracting others that could have taken us beyond the scope of purposes of this book. We have earlier co-edited and given an Introduction to a significant number of readings on ritual in P. J. Stewart and A. Strathern *Ritual* (Ashgate Publications 2010). We also wish to draw to the special attention of our readers the five sizeable volumes of books under the general title of *Ritual Dynamics and the Science of Ritual* published by Harrassowitz Verlag under the general editorship of Axel Michaels in 2010–11.

We wish to thank the many people that have discussed Ritual and Ritual Studies with us over the decades, especially those who have been authors in our Journal of Ritual Studies (www.pitt.edu/~strather/journal.htm) that we co-edit and in the book series that we also co-edit with Carolina Academic Press (www.pitt.edu/~strather/newmonogrph.htm). We thank also the many colleagues who have invited us to present lectures on our work in this field of study, for example, in Norway, Scotland, United States, Taiwan, Australia, New Zealand and China. Also, we thank Ms Catherine Rodgers for her assistance in helping us with the overall production of the typescript of the manuscript for this book. We wish to acknowledge also the very helpful comments that were made on our manuscript through the stages of peer-review process. And finally our thanks to all the many people over the years in our fieldwork areas in the Pacific, Asia and Europe for their insights and explanations about their ritual practices.

About the authors

Dr. Pamela J. Stewart (Strathern) and Prof. Andrew Strathern are a wife-and-husband research team in the Department of Anthropology, University of Pittsburgh, and have been, respectively, Visiting Research Fellow and Visiting Professor, Department of Anthropology, University of Durham, England. They are also Research Associates in the Research Institute of Irish and Scottish Studies, University of Aberdeen, Scotland, and have continuously been Visiting Research Fellows at the Institute of Ethnology, Academia Sinica, Taipei, Taiwan during parts of every year from 2002 to 2013. They were the joint 2012 DeCarle Distinguished Lecturers at University of Otago, Dunedin, New Zealand.

They have published over 45 books and over 200 articles on their research in the Pacific (mainly Papua New Guinea and the South-West Pacific region, e.g. Samoa and Fiji), Asia (mainly Taiwan, and also including Mainland China and Japan), and Europe (primarily Scotland, Ireland and the European Union countries in general); and also New Zealand and Australia. Their most recent co-authored books include *Witchcraft, Sorcery, Rumors, and Gossip* (Cambridge University Press, 2004); *Kinship in Action: Self and Group* (Prentice Hall, 2011) and *Peace-Making and the Imagination: Papua New Guinea Perspectives* (University of Queensland Press, 2011). Their recent co-edited books include *Exchange and Sacrifice* (Carolina Academic Press, 2008) and *Religious and Ritual Change: Cosmologies and Histories* (Carolina Academic Press, 2009). Their current research includes the topics of Cosmological Landscapes, Religious Conversion and Change, Ritual Studies, Political Peace-making, Comparative Anthropological Studies of Disasters; and Language, Culture and Cognitive Science.

Their webpages, listing publications and other scholarly activities, are: www.pitt.edu/~strather/ and www.StewartStrathern.pitt.edu/.

1

Introduction: Problems of definition

'I can't define it, but I know it when I see one' is a last resort remark made sometimes to deal with a complex issue of definition. This has sometimes been the outcome of debates about the definition of ritual. A helpful approach, however, is to consider first what we mean by 'definition'. Does a definition have to be 'hard and fast' or can it be 'fuzzy'? What are the results of either approach? Which is most useful?

Certain characteristics have often been invoked, for example, that ritual implies formality, regularity, stereotyping, special uses of language and communicative gestures and sanctions concerning its correct performance. These are all empirical criteria for inspection, but the overall problem here is 'where do we draw the line' and say that 'this is ritual and that is not'? To deal with this conundrum, we need to stand back and reflect that ritual is not a 'thing', but a term for processes and events that have a particular place in social life. There are problems also of definition in the terms we have used above roughly to indicate the field of ritual, for example, the term 'formality' (see, e.g. Irvine in Duranti, 2001). Our solution, or approach to the solution, of the definitional problem follows in the spirit of Catherine Bell's treatments of it (Bell, 1992, 1997). We are concerned with ritual as practice and performance rather than as an ideal or notional category, and therefore with 'ritualization' as a process that gives special values to actions. And we use the concept of 'framing' to discuss how some behavioural processes are explicitly set off from others as a way of emphasizing values associated with them and endowing them with meanings. We will discuss at various points in this book some earlier theories in the light of this approach, from Durkheim onwards, including Victor Turner, and others. Here we will begin with the work of Roy Rappaport, and Catherine Bell herself. We also note here the use of the term 'ritualization' in ethological studies (Lorenz, 1966; Eibl-Eibesfeldt, 1970; Hinde, 1972, 1987), and briefly compare this arena of thinking with the ideas of theorists such as Catherine Bell. Bell saw ritualization as an intensifying strategy that could be used in various contexts, while the ethologists have related it primarily to appeasement in the face of aggression. Bell's definition is broad, the ethologist's is specific. Our own concept of framing picks out the communicative functions of making distinctions and giving value to actions.

Roy A. Rappaport on ritual: Meaning, truth and participation

We begin with some points from the work of Roy Rappaport. Rappaport's major fieldwork was conducted in 1962–63 among the Tsembaga, a group of some 200 people speaking the Maring Language on the fringes of the Central Highlands of Papua New Guinea (Rappaport, 1968, pp. 12–14). Both warfare and peace-making among the Maring were regulated by precise sequences of action recognizable as rituals, marked in particular at times of transition between states of hostility and peaceful interrelations between groups. In his ethnography and his later extensive theorizing Rappaport sought to understand the place of ritual actions in social life generally. In his 1999 book he specified some characteristics of ritual that he saw as distinctive and important. These were: that ritual is a type of *performance*; that in it the acts are *formal* and relatively *invariant*, governed by *convention*, and carrying meanings that perhaps can only be expressed in *ritual form* (Rappaport, 1999, pp. 23–34). Invariance and formality are central to this definitional set. Rappaport realized that these are not absolute features, but variable.

It is necessary in fact to acknowledge conflict, reform, and shifts in values. If we return to the point that ritual is a performance, we can see that performances may vary. Rappaport further distinguishes rituals from theatre, again noting that the distinction is not total. He argues that in rituals all those present are *participants*, whereas in theatre there is a separation between *performers* and their *audiences* (p. 39). It is arguable, however, that audiences and performers are linked in both rituals and theatrical shows, and that there are ritual elements in theatre (see Schechner, 1985). Some performances, too, may be more successful than others, or may fail altogether.

Several other issues in Rappaport's discussion must be noted here. Rappaport, in his 1999 book, declared that rituals were not efficacious in a physical sense (p. 46). Here, he was following Edmund Leach in viewing rituals as aesthetic acts marking customary identities, distinct from technical actions (p. 47, referring to Leach, 1954, pp. 12–13, reprinted in Stewart and Strathern eds, 2010, pp. 123–31). This distinction between technical acts and ritual acts is based on the idea that technical acts display an obvious means – end relationship, whereas ritual acts refer to hidden, occult, forces that are hypothesized by the performers. Rappaport himself notes that this idea seems negated by the frequent finding that people call their rituals 'work' (Maring *kongung*, see the Melpa *kongon*, from the Mt. Hagen area south of the Maring, see Stewart, Strathern and Trantow, 2011) the same term used for making a garden or for a garden itself (p. 47). Still, he would argue that the work of making a garden differs from ritual work, and that the people themselves would recognize this difference. He refers further to the point that magical actions in rituals are accompanied by verbal specifications which depend on a belief in the power of words themselves, enhanced by stereotypical forms of utterance and style (pp. 49–50). Ritual communication is thus, Rappaport suggests, marked out clearly from other modes of communication by style (or aesthetics in Leach's terms).

In Rappaport's view, what ritual communicates is not power over things but information about the performers' own physical states, or previously encoded information that is regarded as canonical and unchanging, as a form of truth presented as 'sacred'. He refers back here to the Maring, among whom aspects of the *kaiko* festivals take a canonical and invariant form and others are variable and self-referential. Pigs must be sacrificed to spirits in customary (canonical) ways, but when and how many pigs are killed depends on the performers' intentions and capacities (self-referential) (pp. 52–53).

Rappaport was greatly interested in the issue of canonical elements in liturgical orders, rituals arranged in accordance with ideas of hierarchy and truth. He distinguished between low-, middle- and higher-order meanings. He defined low-order meanings as those with obvious semantic references in the physical world, for example, terms for animals such as 'dog'. Middle-order meanings, he suggests, display similarities among phenomena, and their linguistic modality is metaphor. Higher-order meanings reach to conceptions of unity or identity between beings in the world (pp. 71–72). In his discussions of the Maring *kaiko*, Rappaport is concerned mostly with the self-referential (or indexical) messages that are communicated by decorations, numbers of dancers, numbers and qualities of pigs killed and so on, displaying the strength of groups in an 'epideictic' manner for all to see and assess, as well as to the performers themselves. These self-referential meanings can also contain metaphorical messages based on the appearance of decorations and the health of people's bodies, which for the people reveal the state of connection between the performers and their ancestral spirits. They may further encode ideas of unity of being within the wider ecological cosmos to which the Maring see themselves as belonging. In this way, the *kaiko* may express all three levels of meaning that Rappaport categorizes.

A final feature of Rappaport's treatment springs from what we may call a processual approach to the *kaiko* as a form of ritual practice. The information and meanings that are presented in the *kaiko* change the political and ecological situations of the participants. Specifically, Rappaport argues that the *kaiko*, as a ritual performance, changes analogic to digital values. Before the *kaiko* the strength of a group may be variably interpreted and seen as fluid or uncertain (= analogic). After a given *kaiko* the group is seen as strong or weak in accordance with how well it performed (= digital). In a broader sense, the *kaiko* also marks a digital transition between war and peace between clusters of clan groups. For long periods of a ritually established truce, people would make large gardens and raise pigs. When these were killed in the *kaiko* and gifts of pork made to allies in previous rounds of fighting, the group would be ready to enter into new conflicts and fighting. The presence of allies at a *kaiko* and their participation in the dancing also acted as a 'digital' promise of renewed support in such a resurgence of fighting (Rappaport, 1968, p. 195). This point underlines what we may call in contemporary analytical terms the strongly *embodied* character of communication in the *kaiko* and in rituals generally (see Strathern and Stewart, 1998, reprinted in Stewart and Strathern, eds, 2010, pp. 83–97).

Rappaport's contributions to the study of ritual were broadly based and fundamental. Updating the discussion of these contributions here, we note three further points. First, studies of ritual practices today take into account not only variation but also creativity and innovation. This is in line with a general shift towards the study of change as distinct from continuity. In reality, however, change and continuity always coexist and the relationship between invariant and variant factors is an important arena to study. Second, the question of the efficacy of rituals has come to the fore in theorizing, and within this enquiry it is important to understand the people's own view of the world and the forces that make it operate, occult or not (see the studies in *Journal of Ritual Studies* 24 [1 and 2] 2010). This kind of enquiry tends to break down the putative distinction between the technical and the ritual domains. Third, embodiment theory, as remarked on above, is significant nowadays in understanding rituals. The embodied participation of persons in rituals not only influences them in bodily ways but becomes the actual vehicle by which metaphorical meanings are created and credited with efficacy (see, e.g. Strathern and Stewart, 2011).

We will return to these three points at various sites within the book. We now turn to the writings of Catherine Bell.

Catherine Bell's work: On ritualization and meaning

Like Rappaport, Catherine Bell was concerned to deal with definitional questions relating to the concept of ritual, and also to turn these questions in a novel, action-oriented, direction. She approached this problem first in her 1992 book, *Ritual Theory, Ritual*

Action, seeking to resolve philosophical problems created through the binary distinction (in the English language) between thought and action (Bell, 1992, p. 6), stemming from the eighteenth-century trend towards the search for scientific knowledge (ibid.). Her meaning is that abstract thought as science was removed from action, so bringing about the binary duality which she sought to overcome. She proposes the concept of 'ritualization' as a way of acting, and is particularly interested in ritual as a mode of exerting power in shifting and ambiguous contexts (p. 8), where absolute control is not in evidence, and both 'consent and resistance' may be in play (ibid.). Whereas ritual may seem to call for a bounded definition involving some essence or thing-like characteristics, 'ritualization' turns us towards processes that people bring into being and so transform action in certain directions that stress their authoritative character. This idea ties in with ideas expressed by Maurice Bloch (e.g. Bloch, 1989, reprinted in Stewart and Strathern, eds, 2010, pp. 53–82; Bloch, 2005). Bloch was especially concerned with what constitutes the authoritative features of ritual acts, instancing song, dance and rhetoric as important instruments of communication in this regard, and a general attitude of deference toward ancestors, and tradition as a means of deflecting the intentions of ritual actors onto figures of authority.

In her later book, *Ritual: Perspectives and Dimensions* (1997), Bell takes up a list of features of 'ritual-like activities' (p. 138). She stresses early on the significance of the ways people move their bodies and improvise actions, having first described contexts where actions are more fixed in pattern. She picks out *formalism, traditionalism, invariance, rule-governance, sacral symbolism* and *performance* as important topics. Formality involves the use of conventional modes of action, which are harder putatively to disrupt and may carry aesthetic appeal, and which construct and exchange 'face' between people, as in the theories of Erving Goffman (Goffman, 1967; Bell, 1997, p. 141) regarding greetings. The words in these greetings go with bodily gestures, as happens also in table etiquette, and they follow patterns of dominance, hierarchy and equality in the society (for a good example see Duranti, 2009, pp. 188–213). Formality and conscious formalism tend further to go with traditionalism and relative invariance of forms of action. Traditionalism is a conscious appeal to tradition, and, Bell indicates, can entail the exact repetition of earlier activities, their adaptation in some new circumstances, or even the creation of actions that evoke elements from the past (Bell, p. 145). This last category implies the 'invention of tradition' argument that engaged scholars for a while, especially when looking at the construction of symbols of ethnicity or nationhood (e.g. Hobsbawm and Ranger, eds, 1983). Even in such cases of supposed invention, the materials for invention may be taken from traditions or may conform to broad culture-historical patterns that carry easy acceptance and convey values of respect. Academic regalia may be of this kind, in cases where a new university or college is formed and requires academic dress of its own. Coats of arms of titled families have all had to be created at one time, but their structure is also laid down by rules. The link between values and traditionalism is illustrated by Bell by reference to the teachings of Confucius on *li*, ritual or proper forms of ceremony (p. 147). Bell also notes that recently adopted customs often become swiftly referred to as having 'always' been practiced (p. 150). We ourselves have encountered a humorous claim by a colleague at a conference that if something has been done once before, it's a tradition (when you do it the second time).

Invariance is sometimes highlighted, Bell says, as the most important aspect of ritual actions, making them appear timeless (and so also traditional). Formalism, in turn, is frequently an imputed mark of invariance. How, then, to distinguish ritual invariance from other kinds of routine behaviour, whether individual or collective? The distinction can be made only if we attribute to ritual some special (and symbolic) value in society, usually but not always associated with a category of religion or legitimate authority. If we compare here factory workers and monks in a monastic order, we can see that the daily activities of both these categories of actors are comparable in terms of the criteria of precision and control that Bell invokes, but the ultimate aims or ends of their activities clearly differ. Factory workers are likely to see their work as a means to the end of making a living. Monks may see their work as producing themselves as servants of God or in service of an ideal of mindfulness, as in the Zen Buddhist example which Bell gives (p. 151). At some deeper level of analysis, it is possible to suggest that there is a convergence or correspondence.

Workers make sacrifices to the spirit of capitalist production; monks make sacrifices to a deity or a way of life itself. The example underlines the difficulty of making hard and fast distinctions between ritual and non-ritual actions. Where values are attached, ritualization of action is likely to follow regardless of what is being produced, a product or a life. Bell usefully mentions here meditation, requiring precision and control, as another context of ritualization that can become subject to contests about its degree of becoming a standard form of ritual as opposed to an exploration of the self (p. 152). These two need not, of course, actually be opposed. And she significantly notes that the shared performance of a ritual induces an awareness of 'simultaneity' (p. 152), which is another aspect of the ritual process linked to social values of solidarity and identity.

As a further note here, this discussion of invariance does not negate the fact that rituals do change, both in details and in their main form, over time. Even if they are seen by the actors as standing within tradition but outside of history, they are nevertheless products of history and are themselves also agents of historical processes of both continuity and transformation. Thus, rule-governance (Bell, p. 153) is a feature of rituals that is widely shared across the whole spectrum of social actions; but, again, rules do change, because human actors change them for their own purposes. The forms taken by rituals are also certainly shared by other activities, such as boxing (Bell, p. 153) and play. Here, the boundaries can be productively blurred, since both sport and play exhibit clear dimensions of ritualized action. The examples of sumo-wrestling in Japan and football cheerleaders in the United States come readily to mind.

Sacral symbolism is an obvious distinguishing marker of ritualization, because it indexes encompassing values and explicitly creates an arena that is separated from others not considered sacred. Historical sites of significant battles or disasters are likely to be symbolized in this way, to a good extent because of losses of life at them and what these losses meant to kinsfolk or a nation. Pursuing her concept of ritualization as a key to understanding such phenomena, Bell rightly points out that even if an item such as a flag becomes a symbol of the nation and may be thought of as itself sacred, it comes into its symbolic being in practice through the ways in which it is handled, raised, lowered, displayed – or, we may add, draped over the bodies of fallen soldiers brought back to their country for burial after being killed in action overseas.

The final feature that Bell discusses is crucial for theoretical understanding and in a sense summates the other features outlined above, in a context of *practice*. This feature is performance, which implies self-conscious actions in public places. Performance, Bell says (p. 160) involves numerous sensory components that induce a heightened bodily experience among those performing together (and those participating by watching, we may add, a point that is crucial for understanding the extended agency that emerges from media representations of ritual performances such as inaugurations). Bell refers here to 'the dynamics of framing' (p. 160). This is another important phrase. It is the framing, conveyed in words and / or actions, that tells people how to understand an event as a ritual, including the ritual of raising the curtains on a dramatic production that in itself may carry ritual values and may create a sense of 'condensed totality' (p. 161). Bell goes on to remark on 'political theater' that may involve the exercise of violence, such as when governments crack down on protesters or in the historical witch-hunts of Europe (p. 163; see also Stewart and Strathern, 2004). Theatre and ritual clearly overlap in Chinese traditions within which temple festival theatre performances are staged for the birthday of a deity and the deity is said to watch and enjoy the performance. Acrobatic troupes may also be hired for these occasions (Bell, pp. 165–66; see also Sutton, 2003). We ourselves have often watched these occasions in Taiwan, for example, at the birthday celebrations for the goddess Mazu (Stewart and Strathern, 2009). Overall, Bell notes that an appeal is made in these contexts of performance to domains of 'authoritative reality' (p. 169), or what we in our work have denoted as the 'cosmos' (Strathern and Stewart, 2008a, xxvii).

At a theoretical level, two further points can be made. The first point is that performances can vary, and they can also fail (Hüsken ed., 2007). Performances are subject to assessment and judgement. A whole performance may be regarded as an act of divination, to see whether it will please the gods or spirits, or not. The second point is that performance is therefore linked to performativity and efficacy. Performativity refers to the perceived results of a performance, which may include its specific intended purposes and also its secondary consequences, intended or otherwise. These points correspond to the speech-action theory of J. L. Austin, who identified the performativity of utterances in terms of their illocutionary and perlocutionary effects (Austin, 1962). This comparison between speech and ritual is a highly productive one, and leads in turn into the domain of ritual efficacy (see the papers in *Journal of Ritual Studies*, 24 (1 and 2, 2010), as well as reflecting back on the authoritative character of ritualized action.

Briefly, here, efficacy depends on perceptions and on understandings of what a ritualized process of actions is meant to be about. The classic context chosen for discussion of this point centres on healing rituals, where a patient is sick and appeals are made to spirits or deity figures by means of sacrificial offerings, including verbal entreaties, to ensure that the patient recovers. A variant here is shamanic healing, in which the shaman or ritual expert is said to go on a spirit journey to find the cause of a patient's illness and to recover the patient's soul and bring it back into the body. In both cases, the healing concept depends on a concept of an embodied cosmos in which spirit beings interact with people in a perceived social network. Healing, therefore, does not operate simply as a kind of medicine on an individual body. Rather, it is held to operate within the cosmos itself, restoring order by putting substances back into their proper places (see Douglas, 1966). Just as in biomedicine, efficacy depends on numbers of contingent factors that influence how well a medicine works, so in healing practices efficacy depends on the timing, intensity, and skill of the healer's ritual actions. This circumstance provides a context in which healing acts can be evaluated as more or less effective, or not effective at all, necessitating a switch to some other expert or some other type of ritual. Healing, here, is not to be seen as something that operates in a psychological domain separate from the functioning of the patient's body. Instead, in the terms expounded by Geoffrey Samuel, the symbolization of spirit agencies and their involvement has to be seen as contributing to the total organismic restructuring of the patient's body and lifeworld (Samuel, 2010). One ethnography that contributes notably to this theme and adds to it the importance of songs and dreams derived from interactions with the landscape of the rainforest among the Temiar people of Malaysia is Marina Roseman's study of 'healing sounds' (Roseman, 1991).

We move in the next chapter to the history of theorizing about ritual in early stages of the development of social and cultural anthropology in Europe, starting with the work of scholars whose lives spanned the nineteenth and twentieth centuries.

2

Early grand theorists

` Introduction

During the nineteenth and early twentieth centuries in Europe different strands of theorizing contributed to the development of perspectives in anthropology as an academic discipline. Given the prevalence and prestige within the Humanities of the 'Classics', that is, the study of the languages, cultures and histories of places within ancient Greece and Rome, a good deal of anthropological theorizing arose from reconsiderations and reinterpretations of ancient texts that were felt to bear on theories of magic and religion in general. The so-called armchair anthropologists such as Sir Edward Burnett Tylor (e.g. Tylor, 1970) and Sir James George Frazer (e.g. Frazer, 1958) were concerned to draw on a great range of materials from around the world in order to construct synthetic theories of the evolution of human society from its putatively most 'primitive' or original forms. Evolutionary schemes thus provided the framework for their analyses and interpretations of materials. In this context, Greece and Rome figured ambivalently as way-stations: on one hand as the homes of the creators of European civilization, on the other as revealing traces of more primitive forms of belief and ritual still encoded in their practices and artistic productions. One scholar whose work was outstanding in tracing primordial popular elements in ancient Greek religion was Jane Ellen Harrison (e.g. Harrison, 1955). Her approach was through images preserved in material culture such as vases and pots as much as from textual evidence, and these images could be interpreted as relating to ritual activities. This concern with iconography and practice makes Harrison's work in some ways closer to contemporary approaches than Frazer's intellectualist and mentalist approach may seem to be. While it may appear that Frazer's enterprise was to explain magical and religious ideas, Harrison could then be seen to be more engaged with ritual as such. Her work would then be comparable to that of William Robertson Smith, who, however, took his intellectual departure from the study of Hebrew and Arabic materials as these sprang from biblical scholarship. Robertson Smith became famous for his theory of sacrifice as communal sharing with deity figures – in other words, he explained it primarily in social rather than intellectualist or cognitive terms as Frazer did with his materials on magic and religion. His work in turn clearly shared features with that of a different and independent set of thinkers in France, centred on Emile Durkheim, notably Marcel Mauss (e.g. 1990), Henri Hubert (e.g. Hubert and Mauss, 1964) and Robert Hertz (e.g. 1960). Durkheim is perhaps best known for his theory that religion was based on the worship of society itself in sacralized form (Durkheim, 1965), thus producing a purely sociological accounting for it. Such an idea might have suited Frazer's own predominantly secular viewpoint, but it did not turn him aside from his largely mentalist mode of analysis. These two traditions, which we may roughly label the intellectualist versus the sociological paradigms, have persisted into contemporary times; but we will also show that they interpenetrate each other and are not mutually exclusive.

Robertson Smith, for example, (see, e.g. Smith, 1969; and Segal, 1995), argued quite persuasively that the original form of animal sacrifice was an act of commensal sharing between the community of celebrants and their object of worship, the deity. This ritual act was based on the primordial significance of eating together among humans as a mark of solidarity and obligation between the participants. Eating together might be seen as the elementary social act, creating and depending on trust. So far the account may seem to be purely sociological. However, all human actions also depend on ideas. In this case the value given to sharing food must be seen as an idea, albeit one that can be expressed directly in practice without conscious articulation. Moreover, including the deity in the act of sharing is also an ideational act: there has to be a form of metaphysical thinking that facilitates the process. In Mount Hagen society in the Papua New Guinea Highlands the idea was that the spirits of dead kinsfolk shared in pork sacrifices by smelling the pleasant aroma of the meat as it was cooked (see Stewart and Strathern eds, 2008). The explanation of the practice of sacrifice therefore has to lie both in the meanings attributed to sharing food and in the concept of an ancestor as an incorporeal being who still has attributes of personhood. Commensality is at the heart of the social practices that surround the sacrifice; ancestrality is its ideational basis. In addition, of course, there is the significance of the offering itself, in which a life is taken in order to renew life. Ideas and practices are bound together and underpin each other in an indissoluble whole, unless they are forced apart by circumstances of change.

Sir James Frazer on magic

Most overall accounts of Frazer's work tend to foreground his classification of magic into homeopathic and contagious magic under the overall rubric of the supposed Law of Sympathy, with the term Sympathetic Magic covering both homeopathic and contagious magical actions (Frazer, 1958, pp. 13–15, originally published 1922). It is evident here that Frazer has, in scientific fashion, developed a systematic typology or framework of analysis into which all empirical examples will be made to fit. It is also evident, as he himself makes clear, that he presents magic as if it were a kind of science, although empirically wrong in its applications. In other words Frazer starts out from the premise that magic cannot work because both its laws and its practices are based on error. If, however, we ignore this theoretical apparatus of interpretation with which he surrounded the topic, we can see two things. First, many of the examples he gives do fit into his classificatory scheme. Second, the examples can also be interpreted in further ways. Take for instance the practice of making an image of a person and piercing its body parts with a sharp tool (such as a needle) so as to cause an equivalent damage or pain to the person's real body. How is this supposed to work (other than as a device to satisfy desires of the practitioner)? Most likely the image is seen as actually capturing an important part of the life force of the intended victim, so that something in addition to a 'law of sympathy' is in play. In one of Frazer's examples, from Peru, such an effigy is said to have been burned along the pathway that the victim was expected to walk on, and the action was called 'burning his soul' (Frazer, 1958, p. 15). The fat and grain from which the image was made would perhaps contain life force because these elements were vital parts of the food people ate. Shifting from 'homoeopathy' to 'contagion', Frazer's next example, from Malay, allows us to apply the interpretation through life-force ideas very clearly. In this example the magical practitioner (viz. sorcerer) took nail parings, 'hair, eyebrows, spittle . . . enough to represent every part' of the intended victim, and moulded these into a likeness, then scorched it over a lamp for seven nights, declaring that the internal organs of the victim were being burnt (Frazer, p. 15). Here, the principle involved is not simply contiguity or that things that were once in contact can continue to act on each other at a distance as Frazer suggested (p. 12). It is rather that hair and nails and so on continue to embody the life force of the person, hence if these are harmed the person's life will also be threatened. The power in objects such as hair is that they continue to grow over time, hence they become what Mary Douglas (1970) would call 'natural symbols'. While Frazer was concerned to label magic as pseudoscience, later anthropologists have been interested simply in discerning the complexities of logic and of social context in which magical, and religious, practices are embedded. Lévi-Strauss's work on *La Pensée Sauvage* (Lévi-Strauss, 1966) and Stanley Tambiah's work reanalyzing the symbolic logic of Trobriand Islanders' canoe motifs and garden magic (Tambiah, 1968) exemplify these more recent trends.

On the other side of the discussion, Frazer should be credited with bringing conceptual clarity to what was otherwise a somewhat confused jumble of ethnographic reports about magic. (Compare here in general Philsooph, 1995, although the point we make here is our own view.) Moreover, his insights made in passing give us glimpses of his imaginative approach to interpretation of data, as when he argues that Sympathetic Magic in general works by means of an 'impulse being transmitted . . . by means of what we may conceive as a kind of invisible ether' (p. 14). He is inventing here a notion of a field of perceived forces within which magic operates, or obtains its perceived efficacy. What he is referring to is the power of what we might nowadays call the universal relationality or the extended embodiment of social life. This is essentially the same force field that Durkheim identified in the sphere of religion as that of society worshipping itself: or, as we may reformulate this, society creating itself through communication in a charged emotional context of collectivity. Finally here, although Frazer in his role as a follower of science and of the evolutionary theories of society at his time which had absurd consequences when projected onto colonial relations between colonizers and those they colonized, in his role as an anthropologist he reveals clearly his fascination with and respect for untangling the meanings of the myriad indigenous customs that he so painstakingly unearthed and marshalled together in his voluminous scholarly works.

He also understood the social functions of these same customs. In his 'Psyche's Task' (1909, reissued 1927) he undertook a defence of sorts of magic and religion by showing how ideas such as that of 'taboo' were put to work to uphold patterns of chiefly authority and property holding in society. If he thought of magic, from the viewpoint of its practitioners, as a kind of art rather than a science (1958, p. 13), this insight also can be employed to dignify magic rather than to denigrate it (as Frazer did by putting the adjective 'bastard' in front of the noun 'art'), since art surely is one of the finest as well as the oldest capacities of creativity that humans possess; and many matters in social life are negotiated by art and cannot be determined by scientific means. If we strip Frazer's formulations of their pejorative excrescences and extract their interpretive validity, we can see considerable value in his ideas. His project to outline the main characteristics of so-called primitive thought can fruitfully be compared with the similarly grand schemes of Lévy-Bruhl (1926) and Lévi-Strauss (1966), including the point that all three of these authors were intent on retaining the idea of fundamental difference between 'primitive' and 'modern' forms of mentalities, an idea that Jack Goody has effectively critiqued and replaced with his own contrasts between pre-literate and literate cultural order (e.g. Goody, 1977). We do not mean here, by the way, to equate Frazer's ideas in any detail with those of Lévy-Bruhl or of Lévi-Strauss. As might be expected, however, from their historical placement, Frazer's idea of

Sympathetic Magic and Lévy-Bruhl's idea of mystical participation are close to each other and reinforce the primitive versus modern dichotomy, whereas Lévi-Strauss's idea of the 'science of the concrete' (cited in Goody, 1977, p. 5) moves further away from this dichotomy and negates Frazer's denial of the term 'science' to those cultures that he studied. Indeed, Lévi-Strauss goes a step further and argues that myths, and by implication their magico-religious logics, may not have any practical functions at all but may be pure acts of ratiocination. Such a view would not only devalue the anthropologist Malinowski's insistence that myths and rituals meet people's needs in social life (e.g. Malinowski, 1948), but would also bypass Frazer's insistence that magic is instrumental for its participants and should be called Practical Magic, as opposed to the systematization of it into categories such as Frazer himself developed, which he called Theoretical Magic (Frazer, 1958, p. 13).

While reversing Frazer's order of precedence here with deliberate theoretical intent, Pierre Bourdieu made a similar distinction between objectivism (the analyst's construction) and behaviour (the actors' practices), critically citing Ferdinand de Saussure's famous distinction in linguistics between *langue* (language as an objectified entity) and *parole* (speech, actual uses of linguistic forms) (Bourdieu, 1990, cited in Moore and Sanders, 2006, pp. 170–78). Frazer clearly privileged the analyst's perspective as the site of true knowledge. Bourdieu critiques such a view, emphasizing the prior reality of practice and usage.

In another context of his work Frazer re-privileged the views of the actors in relation to the social roles of taboo and magic. Adopting a functionalist perspective that clearly anticipated the work of A. R. Radcliffe-Brown, he described 'Psyche's task' as the work of what he called 'superstition' in establishing order in society. This was in relation to the work of ritual practices and ideas in supporting 'government' (e.g. chiefs, leaders), property (i.e. by taboos); marriage (i.e. by sanctions attached to the breaking of rules); and concern for life (i.e. by fear of the ghosts of the dead). If in all instances we were to substitute the term 'religion' for Frazer's 'superstition', the argument would remain the same, and would not need to be attached to an evolutionary argument about 'superstition' being a left-over remnant from former times. Since in the examples he gives Frazer is in effect giving credit to those who created the customs he describes, it is clear that he was also offering a putative rehabilitation of the character of the 'primitives' or 'savages' whom he spent his lifetime studiously investigating (Frazer, 1927). Indeed, it is our overall suggestion here that, like many of his contemporaries who were fascinated by the discoveries they made in comparative ethnography, Frazer's attitude to the so-called primitive was complex, if not ambivalent. In 'Psyche's Task' he seems finally to have resolved a part of this complexity of attitude by recognizing the social value of customs. Stripped of its mechanistic dark/light oppositions and its use of 'superstition' as a term, Frazer's work begins to emerge, in a way not generally recognized, as a creative forerunner of the synchronic functionalism of the school of 'British' social anthropology (guided in fact by thinkers of Polish, South African, Welsh and Scottish extraction as well as English). The intermediary in this process was Bronislaw Malinowski, who seems to have recognized the significance of Frazer's work in this context. Frazer himself set his argument into the idioms of classical mythology, in which the beautiful Psyche was given four seemingly impossible tasks by the goddess Aphrodite, who was angry that her son Eros had secretly married Psyche. One of these tasks was to sort out a huge heap of seeds of wheat, barley, poppy, beans, lentils and peas. She performed this with the aid of a swarm of friendly ants that took pity on her. Frazer transformed the story further, in likening Psyche's task to sorting out seeds of good and evil in society and setting himself the task of discovering the seeds of good custom in the cross-cultural records he studied so intensively. The figure of Psyche remains intriguing. Is she intended to represent Culture in its historical dimension? Her name, of course, means Soul or Spirit, perhaps indexing the passages of the human spirit through time.

Jane Ellen Harrison and classical studies

Jane Ellen Harrison was a lecturer in Classical Archaeology at Newnham College, Cambridge University, from 1900 onward. Born in 1850, she died in 1928. Her life overlaps considerably, therefore, with that of Frazer, who was born in 1854 and spent much of his life as a Fellow of Trinity College in Cambridge, dying in 1941. Harrison and Frazer, like Robertson Smith, were both proponents of the relatively new methods of comparative and historical enquiry into religious forms that developed in the later years of the nineteenth century and were strengthened by archaeological discoveries. These enquiries gave rise, among many other trends, to approaches to the ritual and historical roots of ancient Greek tragic and comic drama, exemplified in the work of Frances Cornford (1914) and Gilbert Murray (e.g. 1927). Harrison firmly set her perspectives in stressing ritual rather than mythology or literature and in discerning popular and older patterns of cultic action behind the glittering facades of Greek literature, or at least the facades created by Classical scholars. In this regard, she uses Greek literary sources much as Frazer did, drawing *inter alia* on works by Apollodorus and Pausanias, of which Frazer himself made erudite translations and on which he composed scholarly commentaries. But she points out that an understanding of ritual backgrounds leads to a better understanding of the Greek tragic dramas themselves, especially those of Aeschylus (Harrison, 1955, viii). Like Frazer, too, Harrison operates with a historical perspective that sees certain ritual forms as older and more 'primitive' than their later literary presentations. Her approach, however, is sophisticated and is grounded closely in evidence and in the views the ancient Greeks themselves held about their past. She introduces here a distinction between Olympian and Chthonic rituals of sacrifice (1955, vii). The Olympian deities, portrayed in myriad literary sources and notably in the poetic epic works of Homer, were seen as dwelling in the sky or on the summit of the lofty Mount Olympus in Thessaly in northern Greece, a typical way of locating powers in remote and inaccessible locations. Older ritual practices, Harrison argues (1955, ix), were directed towards powers of the earth and its fertility, and the ancient shrines to these powers were later taken over by devotees of the Olympian gods. In her book on *The Religion of Ancient Greece* (n.d.) Harrison suggests that the more ancient forms of ritual can be called Pelasgian, following the account given by the fifth century BCE Greek historian Herodotus, who wrote that: 'Formerly the Pelasgians on all occasions of sacrifice called upon gods, as I know from what I heard at Dodona; but they gave no title nor yet any name to any of them' (Harrison, n.d., p. 16, citing Herodotus, ii, 53 ff.). 'Pelasgian' here is a term for pre-Hellenic populations, and the rituals of these peoples seem to have been directed towards female powers generally and mother-goddess figures, as Robert Graves argued extensively in his two volumes of classical mythology (Graves, 1960, revised edition). Dodona, mentioned here in the citation from Herodotus, was an important oracle shrine which people might go to for consultations, and was very ancient. Herodotus reported the oral history of the priestesses at Dodona, saying that their shrine was associated with a story of two black doves that had flown from Thebes in Egypt and one of them landed at Dodona on an oak tree and declared that a place of divination should be established there. Herodotus argued that this story reflected an actual event in which a slave priestess was taken by Phoenician sailors from Egypt and sold in Thesprotia on the Coast near to Dodona, and later founded the oracle there. Although Herodotus referred to this as a shrine to Zeus, it is thought to have earlier been presided over by Gaia, an Earth-Mother figure, called at Dodona Dione, and this goddess and Zeus of the Spring (Zeus Naios) continued to share the shrine. The power of the oak tree at Dodona was marked in two ways: the priestesses interpreted the rustling of its leaves in order to provide oracular answers; and in the story of Jason and the Argonauts, the ship itself, the Argo, was said to have prophetic power because one of its timbers was made of oak taken from a tree at Dodona that was part of the sacred grove of oaks around the shrine. The shrine was not only very ancient, it also lasted long until Christian times in the Roman empire, until the Emperor Theodosius closed all pagan temples and had the sacred oak cut down.

Frazer devotes several pages to a discussion of the sacred significance of the oak tree in ancient Europe (e.g. Frazer, 1958, pp. 184–86, 770–71, 813, 818); and he begins with a reference to the sanctuary of Zeus at Dodona, noting that the area, in Epirus, is subject to heavy thunderstorms, and that thunder and lightning were seen as marks of Zeus and his power. He refers also to a shrine to Zeus on Mount Lycaeus in Arcadia where a priest dipped an oak branch into a spring as a charm to bring rain (recall here the title of Zeus at Dodona as Zeus of the Spring). Ancient Greek kings, Frazer remarks, sometimes claimed descent from Zeus (presumably because of his numerous supposed liaisons with human females), and so might claim rainmaking powers. Frazer cites examples from Slavic society and from Lithuania, suggesting that the thunder-god in these areas was also associated with the oak, and sacred fires in which oak wood was burnt were kept perpetually alight. Finally, this disquisition allows Frazer to broach one of his central themes, that in ancient Celtic Gaul oak groves were holy places for ritual and that 'the Druids esteemed nothing more sacred than the mistletoe and the oak on which it grew' (p. 185). Frazer's account is innocent, however, of any recognition of the 'Pelasgian' elements of ritual at Dodona. (See Cook, 1915 for an in-depth examination of Zeus.)

The details of this story are significant in a number of ways. First, the history of the shrine at Dodona indicates, in line with Harrison's general argument, that an older shrine to an earth goddess figure was later amalgamated with a shrine to the Olympian god Zeus. If we look more deeply, we also see that the figure of Zeus himself is multiple. The name 'Zeus of the spring' indicates an earth and fertility-linked aspect of the deity. And in Herodotus's account, the shrine was originally set up by a priestess who had come from Thebes in Egypt where Zeus was worshipped, also showing an origin of Zeus as a figure outside of Greece.

Second, it is pertinent to note the extreme importance of landscape and location in ritual practices. Once a shrine is established, if another deity is espoused, this deity's rituals may be grafted onto, or combine with the former ones at the same place. Power belongs as much to the place itself as to a particular deity, because the original choice to make it an oracular shrine must have been prompted by some divinatory signs.

Third, it is important to recognize the narratives of change in religious practices. The history of older and more recent practices at Dodona parallels the later history in Europe of the relationship between pagan and Christian places of worship. In Europe Christianity replaced pagan practices, often with a measure of conflict, but here too Christian holy places were often established in locations where pagan rituals had been held. The extreme version of religious conflict that characterizes the history of Christianity is signalled by the actions of Emperor Theodosius in 391–92 BCE of cutting down the sacred pagan oak tree. Older practices are more like those we find in histories of change in pre-Christian Papua New Guinea, where new ritual practices brought in, perhaps to go with new subsistence practices or new forms of wealth, were simply added to the roster of existing rituals directed to ancestors (see, e.g. Strathern and Stewart, 1999a on the Female Spirit or Amb Kor complex in Mount Hagen, Papua New Guinea).

Returning to the immediate context of Jane Ellen Harrison's work, we may profitably note two further, interrelated points. First, while using extensively surviving literary accounts, Harrison depended particularly on representations of rituals found on objects of material culture, particularly ancient painted vases and jars. The findings of archaeological work were in her time bringing to light much evidence that was previously not available. In a deeper sense, Harrison was also pointing to the connections between art and ritual, as she argued in her book of that title (Harrison, 1951). The representations of ritual and mythological processes in art were not purely aesthetic: they would be expressions of pervasive concerns and cultural themes, and vases and jars might themselves figure in ritual processes. To make a comparison again with Papua New Guinea, art forms there were very prominently a part of ritual practices since they were the materializations or visible revelations of the secret powers at the heart of the rituals themselves; and this point extends notably to the elaborate decorations worn by participants who danced and sang at ritual events (see again Strathern and Stewart, 1999a).

Second, and relatedly, Harrison notes in her short study of *The Religion of Ancient Greece* referred to above that 'Greek mythology is, on the showing of Herodotus, largely the outcome of literature' (p. 15). She cites Herodotus here, but the insight is also her own, and can be extended further. She is saying that Greek composers of literature, using the arts of literacy, systematized and organized a mass of materials; and in particular she notes that the figures of the Olympian deities were made vivid and given form by the epic poets Homer and Hesiod, whose works reveal aspects of pre-literate oral composition and delivery but also abutted into the times when written versions of works were being produced. The broader theoretical context here, following the work of Jack Goody and many others, is that the significance of literacy in changing mental and social processes has been widely debated. Goody has argued that literacy changes modes of thought and conduces to the development of systematic ways of representing the world (e.g. Goody, 1977, 2000, 2010). Although this idea has been critiqued from various angles (e.g. Besnier, 1995), it is reasonable to suggest that Homer and Greek writers after him basically created a pantheon of Olympian deities out of a much wider and historically more complex set of historically layered figures embedded in local ritual practices (Kitts, 1999). It was this set of ritual practices that was the focus of Harrison's work, and her enduring contribution was to show how different the character of Greek religion appears when this level of practice as opposed to literate representations is analyzed.

Harrison's work also resonated with that of Frazer on popular religion, because when she examined the ancient Greek materials she found seasonal rituals of fertility, ideas of animals as spirits, rituals of purification, initiation practices, the gradual anthropomorphizing of spirit entities, sacrificial killings, and sacred marriages, all themes that link the ancient Greeks to old popular ritual practices throughout northern Europe, as well as showing connections with Egypt, the Middle East and Asia. Such an ethnographic picture has to be set against the prominent themes of officialized respect for 'the Greeks' that developed in Europe after the Renaissance, where the images were derived from 'great philosophers' such as Plato and Aristotle, and 'great poets' such as Homer and the tragedians Aeschylus, Sophocles and Euripides, and the classic historians Thucydides and Herodotus – although Herodotus himself, as an astute historian of his day, provided Harrison with her insight about mythology and literature. Harrison also takes us into the debate about the relationship of early Greek rituals to practices of matriarchy and matrilineal descent; or, more generally, into the significance and history of powerful female deity figures such as Pallas Athene, pictured in later mythology as springing from the head of the male supreme deity Zeus (Harrison, 1955, pp. 305–07), but originally seen in different ways with links to goat-figures from Libya and with varying deities said to be her father (Graves, 1960, vol. 1, pp. 44–46).

Harrison's work is also a major forerunner of later trends in Classical Studies (to which Frazer notably also contributed in his time, since he began as a noted Classics scholar and retained his love of Greek and Latin materials) in which study of the Classics has been greatly reinvigorated by a continuous pouring into it of insights from comparative ethnography. The later trend may be said to stem particularly from E. R. Dodds's Sather Lectures on *The Greeks and the Irrational* (Dodds, 1951), in which Dodds identified many of the same practices that Harrison unearthed and set these against the picture of the Greeks as the founders in European history of rationality and science. However, Harrison did not speak of the practices she discussed as 'irrational'. She did refer to them as a 'lower stratum', utilizing 'primitive' ritual motifs (1955, p. ix), but her whole discussion makes it clear that she regarded these themes as having deep and continuing spiritual meaning, particularly in their feminine aspects (see, e.g. 1955, p. 313; and compare the eulogy of her work in Carpentier, 1994).

The reinvigoration of Classical studies by way of ethnography and anthropology is also a testament to the power and appeal of myth and ritual. Of a large corpus of works, and with no particular suggestion of priority of significance, we mention here Jean-Pierre Vernant's *The Universe, The Gods and Men* (2001), Georges Dumézil's *Archaic Roman Religion*, vols 1 and 2 (1996), Judith M. Barringer's *Art, Myth, and Ritual in Classical Greece* (2008), Mark D. Stansbury-O'Donnell's *Looking at Greek Art* (2011) and Eric Csapo and Margaret C. Miller's edited volume *The Origins of Theater in Ancient Greece and Beyond: From Ritual to Drama* (2007). Barringer's title seems to carry over a resonance from Harrison's *Ancient Art and Ritual* (1951), although Harrison's works do not appear in her bibliography. Another work, *The 'Orphic' Gold Tablets and Greek Religion*, edited by Radcliffe G. Edmonds III, does, however, include *Prolegomena to the Study of Greek Religion* in its references and the value of Harrison's work is noted in it (e.g. p. 234). Csapo and Miller, in their General Introduction, acknowledge the early influence of Harrison among the group they call 'the Cambridge Ritualists', and they consider whether this set of scholars, including Gilbert Murray, emphasized the role of ritual elements in tragic drama too greatly; and they also note that some scholars think that 'reducing' drama to 'ritual' diminishes our sense of the creativity of drama. Suffice it to note here, first that Harrison shows a deep sensibility with regard to the poetics of both Greek literature and the ritual forms she painstakingly elaborated, and second that 'modern', or contemporary, studies of ritual do not see it as static or uncreative – quite the reverse. Csapo and Miller go on to make a thorough update of the discussion, both in terms of ritual theory and in relation to Harrison and her work. They note: 'The categories of ritual and drama are not so much divided as joined by a continuum' (Csapo and Miller, 2007, p. 4), and they see Greek dramas as closer to the ritual end of the continuum than some other examples. They cite the performance theories of Richard Schechner (1985) in which the continuum is explored; and to this we may add an example of our own writing on Papua New Guinea (Strathern and Stewart, 1997).

The controversy between Harrison (and her colleagues) and the 'Anti-Ritualists' seems to have turned crucially on the question of whether the underlying, or earlier, form of what became the ancient Greek drama, was that of a ritual cycle in which the spirit of the old year was chased out or sacrificed in favour of the New Year, symbolized in one representation by the figure of the deity Dionysos. In *Ancient Art and Ritual* Harrison discusses seasonal rites in general, moves to popular Spring festivals in Greece, and then shifts to drama. She points to the importance of the Chorus in Greek drama. The Chorus players sang and danced in the orchestra area of the theatre-complex, and the early form of dancing of the chorus, she suggests, was the dithyramb, a dance in praise of the advent of the New Year in the form of a child or youth. The dithyramb celebrated a *dromenon*, an event, like an initiation, and when spectators were added to the event, the event became a *drama*, Harrison suggests. The *agon*, or struggle which the Greek dramas portrayed was originally a struggle between Winter and the New Year, and the clash between them brought about a *peripeteia*, reversal of ritual role, followed by the *epiphany* of a young god replacing the old one. Harrison argues (1951, p. 139) that this old ritual form remained as a shadow in the plot structures of the Greek dramas as they developed in the artistic hands of Aeschylus, Sophocles and Euripides. Whether the account is exactly correct perhaps cannot be settled. However, her general point that drama arose out of ritual performances seems well supported, and certainly gives depth to the meaning of the term 'drama', especially given the later work of Victor Turner on ritual performances as therapeutic dramas among the Ndembu people of Zambia (e.g. Turner, 1967) and his general discussions of performance as a category of analysis (Turner, 1985a,

1986). In Turner's therapeutic model of ritual the drama consists of a process of discovering the cause of misfortune or sickness through a struggle, and the resolution of the struggle through the recreation of order. Clearly, this is not the same *dromenon*, or event, as Harrison postulated for ancient Greece. It is, nevertheless, a model of the same order as Harrison's: an underlying plot, theme, or motif that gives meaning to a whole process.

Emile Durkheim and Arnold van Gennep

These two eminent figures in the history of anthropology contributed in obvious ways to scholarship on ritual, and their basic ideas have been used and re-used and examined critically many times. For this reason we give here only the main points needed to bring our narrative forward.

Durkheim lived 1858–1917, thus overlapping considerably with the lifespan of Frazer (1854–1941). Their traditions of thought were markedly different, except that both accepted the principles of social evolution and sought to understand the fundamentals of human behaviour in the records of 'primitive' peoples. Durkheim was also concerned, like Frazer, to make distinctions between magic and religion. His approach to answering questions was different from Frazer's. Frazer sought to outline mental principles or laws that he thought guided individual actions. Durkheim instead worked with ideas of the collectivity, of the 'conscience collective' (collective consciousness and morality), and of solidarity. Frazer's focus was on culture, Durkheim's was on society.

Durkheim's main contribution to the theory of ritual was made in his book, *The Elementary Forms of the Religious Life* (Durkheim, 1965, originally published in French in 1915). His theoretical approach in this work was consistent with all of his earlier ideas, and centred on the idea that the form of society provides us with the explanation for patterns of behaviour. In terms of ethnographic materials he chose to concentrate on Australian Aboriginal cases, on which in his time new data were being provided. He chose these cases because for him they exemplified very simple states of society and religion, uninfluenced by other societies. Durkheim thought that in this way he would be able to discover the essential link between religion and society. In particular, he chose to emphasize the custom of totemism, whereby groups identified themselves with emblems, derived from their world of experience and relating to their landscape and the creatures living in it. In Durkheim's view, group members worshipped their totem in ritual celebrations, and since the totem symbolized the group this meant that the group was worshipping itself in a cosmologized form. We can see the logic of Durkheim's argument here and how it fits with his aim of privileging the category of 'society' as the explanation of behavior rather than as something which in itself requires explanation. However, what we may think of as 'culture' seems to be left out. Totemic beliefs and practices are very complex and deal with issues of reproduction and secret power. In other words totems are complex ritual figures in their own right, products of the religious imagination and the construction of overall values in the society. In worshipping their totems, people may indeed be in a sense worshipping 'themselves' and 'society'; but these terms gain meaning from the imaginative constructs that people bring to bear on their lives. Durkheim's arguments contain a fundamental truth. The idea of God, for example, represents the highest ideals of those who construct a profile of their deity; but this idea may be infused with many different elements of a cultural and historical kind.

Nevertheless, Durkheim's influence on the study of religion and ritual has been profound. He located the study firmly in the realm of the collective and the social rather than in individual psychology, giving an autonomous place for theorizing about religion as a social practice. He also stressed the importance of participation and experience in rituals as constitutive of their hold on people. In this regard he anticipated later versions of embodiment and emplacement theory, as well as the anthropology of experience generally. However, he tended to over-stress 'society' as the means of explaining all mental categories, such as those of space and time. One very productive influence he had was in drawing around him a band of fellow-thinkers such as Henri Hubert, Robert Hertz, and Marcel Mauss. Mauss's classic study of 'the gift' as a ritual practice has generated long-lasting and fertile discussions surrounding the concept of 'the spirit of the gift', which, interestingly enough, he drew from Maori materials (Mauss, 1990 [1923], see Strathern and Stewart, 2008b). Durkheim's ideas and approach became foundational for the development of British social anthropology through the work of Alfred Reginald Radcliffe-Brown (see Kuper, 1977). Of course, his insistence on a realm of the social as entirely separate from the realm of psychology is negated by studies of group psychology. Jason Throop and Charles D. Laughlin have also re-examined the role of psychology in the processes of group effervescence that Durkeim made central in his own approach (Throop and Laughlin, 2002). Finally, here, it is pertinent to note that, in line with his overall predilections for the social, Durkheim distinguished magic from religion, saying that magical acts were individual, whereas religion was collective and constituted by 'churches'. Magical acts, however, may also be conducted on a collective ritual plane. Durkheim further argued that all social life was divided into realms of the sacred and the profane, and religion dealt with the sacred. This would tend to leave magic in the 'profane' category, but most writers have recognized a hybrid domain of the 'magico-religious', since religion and magic are often blended together in terms of their ultimate aims.

Critiques and appreciations of Durkheim's work abound, testifying to his enduring relevance. Examples are: Bell, 1997, pp. 24–26; Moore, 2012, pp. 42–54; Rappaport, 1999, pp. 170–75, 373–81. Bell's remarks are largely appreciative, but she notes that Durkheim overplayed the equation of religion and society. Moore carefully expounds Durkheim's complex notion of the 'conscience collective' (collective consciousness/moral sensibility) as the sentiment supporting social solidarity. Rappaport comments on Durkheim's argument that categories of thought are derived from social forms, pointing out (following work by Rodney Needham) that if such categories are at the back of everything they should be manifest in all domains of action not only in religion. The problem here is that in some sense religion and society may indeed be 'the same' or identical, depending on how they are defined. Jens Kreinath has made a particularly insightful contribution here, pointing out that Durkheim concentrated on ritual in his expositions and was able to make good use of the photographic images of rites practiced by

Australian Aboriginal peoples. Kreinath thus successfully associates Durkheim with what later became known as practice theory (Kreinath, 2012a).

While Durkheim's writings fed into the more workaday theorizing of Radcliffe-Brown, the models of process supplied by Arnold van Gennep were taken up productively by Victor Turner. Van Gennep's work was also much more specific than Durkheim's, centring on initiation rites and producing a general three-stage model of these which fed into a picture of how society is constituted and its roles structurally reproduced over time.

Van Gennep's study of Rites of Passage appeared in French in 1908, and seems not to have been translated into English till 1960. In his Introduction to this translation (made by Monika B. Vizedom and Gabrielle L. Caffee), Solon Kimball situates van Gennep in the Durkheimian flow of work. Van Gennep, for instance, made a sharp distinction between religion and magic and between the sacred and the profane. In a fashion similar to Durkheim's study of Australian Aboriginal religion, van Gennep noted (1960, p. 2) that in some societies all passages of individuals from one status to another entailed ideas of the sacred. His basic model of such passages was (1) separation, (2) transition (or 'margin') and (3) incorporation. The individual was first separated from their former status and then entered into a sacred state of marginality, finally being incorporated again into the profane domain. He generalized as follows: 'The life of an individual in any society is a series of passages from one age to another and from one occupation to another' (p. 3). Rituals are the ways in which such passages are actually brought into effect. Van Gennep cited life-cycle rituals as the prime locus of passages; but, quite interestingly, he also seeks to include periodic rituals such as seasonal festivals in his scheme, although it is not clear whether the tripartite scheme can be applied to these.

Van Gennep also took as his imaginative model for rites of passage generally the concept of territorial passage (p. 15), noting that such passages are often marked by rituals since boundaries between groups are strongly marked. He further notes that boundaries are marked socially by setting up posts, upright rocks, or gateways (airport immigration and custom zones are the contemporary equivalents here). Those who cross these boundaries are for the time being, he says, in a sacred zone. Doorways and thresholds mark this difference, and those who pass through them are in the ritual state of the edge or margin of the sacred, possibly having undergone rites of purification in preparation (a vestige of which is found, we may note, in rules to take off one's shoes before entering a temple). Van Gennep called the separation rituals pre-liminal rites and those during the stage of transition liminal ones, a vocabulary which Victor Turner was later to take up and explore in detail (Van Gennep, 1960, p. 21). The doorway might also be the place of a guardian deity; or of some special object. Van Gennep notes that when an Orthodox male Jew went through a house's main door he touched with a finger of his right hand the mezuzzah, 'a casket attached to the doorpost which contains a piece of paper or a ribbon upon which is written or embroidered the sacred name of God (Shaddai)' (p. 24), saying 'The Lord shall preserve thy going out and thy coming in from this time forth for evermore' (ibid.). The phrase is reminiscent of the blessing by the priest or minister that concludes a Christian church service as the worshippers leave the church and re-enter the ordinary (viz. 'profane' in Durkheimian terms) world outside.

Van Gennep proceeds to run through a dazzling series of examples illustrating the cross-cultural reality of his structural model, which goes well beyond the context of initiation rites where it is usually, or predominantly employed, using materials from comparative analysts such as Robertson Smith, Edward Westermarck, Frazer and Ernest Crawley ('The Mystic Rose'). Anticipating Mauss, he writes: 'Exchanges have a direct constraining effect: to accept a gift is to be bound to the giver' (p. 29). He saw exchange as an act of incorporation, thus perhaps recognizing that his tripartite model might be found only partly in some contexts, although gifts are often accompanied by greetings which function as indexes of entry into a new relationship of solidarity. Although the methodology here is one of very broad comparative reference, in terms of his theory, van Gennep asserted that in all cases we need to look at the total context in which customs take place. In this view, then, he became a forerunner of the structural-functional approach.

When he comes to initiation rites themselves, van Gennep is entirely consistent. On circumcision practices, he notes that these are acts of separation and also of incorporation into a special category of people among whom this bodily mark is a permanent statement of identity (p. 72). This explanation is sufficient for him, and he classes circumcision along with all other practices of modifying the body, for example, by hair-cutting, ear-piercing, septum-piercing, tattooing, scarifying and the like (p. 72). He proceeds with a discussion of initiation, starting à la Durkheim with the relatively recent reports of Australian Aboriginal practices. Quoting the Kurnai studied by A. W. Howitt and Lorimer Fison, he notes the statement that the initiated boys are cut off from their past and their ties to their mothers, and aggregated into the society of men (p. 75). The novice may be considered dead and then be resurrected. Sacred objects may be shown to him, such as masks or bull-roarers (p. 79); or sacred stones, as with initiates into the Female Spirit ritual in Mount Hagen, Papua New Guinea (Strathern and Stewart, 1999a). In a number of places van Gennep makes determined reference to parallels between Christian practices such as baptism and non-Christian customs, for example, between the Kwakiutl practice of exorcising a spirit in order to move a child on its life's pathway and baptism (p. 76); and between the Navaho practice of touching novices with ears of maize corn or sprinkles of corn meal and once again with baptism. Of course, naming and renaming are often vital parts of the creation of a new identity. Van Gennep's comparisons are meant to be structural, to show parallel functions in different cultural modalities, and to place all practices on an even plane in respect of structural commonalities. He includes also an exposition of the ancient Greek mysteries at Eleusis, for which he relies on Jane Ellen Harrison's work (*Prolegomena*, 1955). These rituals involved rites of separation, purification, and the transport of a sacred image connected to agriculture to Eleusis itself. Inside the walls of the enclosure at Eleusis initiates were shown an image of the rising of the earth-maiden, Kore, out of the ground, and were then reborn into the sacred world (pp. 90–91). Van Gennep goes on once more to compare those patterns with the ideas of death and rebirth in Catholic baptism and in the consecration of Catholic virgins as brides of Christ.

The scope of van Gennep's examples is very broad, and he constantly makes intercontinental comparisons, for example, between Australia and Arabia (p. 186). Overall he stresses that rituals mark gender separations and separations between sacred and profane realms. He also notes how ritual for one type of transition may be modelled on ones for another, for example, initiation and marriage. He remarks in the last paragraph of the book on the joining together of the human life cycle and wider cosmic processes in some societies (p. 194). And his main conclusion points clearly forward to structural-functional analyses: 'Our interest', he writes, 'lies not in the particular rituals but in their essential significance and their relative positions within ceremonial wholes – that is, their order' (p. 191).

Social order was the main focus of the work of Radcliffe-Brown, whose views are often both paired with and contrasted with those of Bronislaw Malinowski. We turn to these two writers and their fellow-scholars of ritual in the next chapter.

3

The fieldwork revolution: Malinowski, Radcliffe-Brown and Boas

'**A**rmchair anthropology' was replaced in the early twentieth century by fieldwork and the intensive detailed analysis of particular societies: for example, Malinowski's Trobrianders, Radcliffe-Brown's Andaman Islanders, Franz Boas's Kwakiutl. Malinowski's functionalism took a psychological turn, embracing the individual and the emotions as well as the place of ritual in society. Radcliffe-Brown's austere concentration on social functions after the manner of Durkheim nevertheless took account of sentiments, meanings, and emotions. Boas's work, which gave rise to the holism of 'the four fields approach' in American cultural anthropology, made a particular contribution to the study of language in society and to the collection of texts from informants rather than to the theory of ritual as such, although he obtained rich material on the famous Kwakiutl potlatch rituals, which we will consider here and compare with competitive ritualized exchanges known as *moka* in Mount Hagen, Papua New Guinea (Strathern and Stewart, 2000; Strathern, 2007).

Malinowksi's work on magical spells (criticized and built on by S. J. Tambiah), and Radcliffe-Brown's work on ritualized expressions such as weeping will be highlighted for their enduring significance, even as their overall theories of society have been partially overtaken by historical changes in the societies anthropologists study.

The so-called armchair theorists in anthropology were not
opposed, of course, to fieldwork. Indeed, they depended on the
growing work of ethnographers around the world, often on the
writings of Christian missionaries who saw such work as essential
to their missionizing task of cross-cultural understanding and
transformation. They overlapped in time with expeditions such as the
Cambridge expeditions to the Torres Straits led by A. C. Haddon in
1888 and 1898; and with those who became leaders in British social
anthropology, notably Bronislaw Malinowski, and A. R. Radcliffe-
Brown, identified with a stress on the importance of fieldwork as
a major source of anthropological knowledge and theory. Frazer, for
example, wrote an appreciative foreword to Malinowski's *Argonauts
of the Western Pacific* (Frazer, 1922 in Malinowski, 1922); and he
was no doubt well aware of Radcliffe-Brown's work from the time
that the latter was a Research Fellow in Trinity College in Cambridge,
Frazer's own College (see, e.g. Ackerman, 1987, p. 339, n. 19).

In spite of this overlap, however, differences of perspective do
emerge between Frazerian anthropological writings and those of
Malinowski and Radcliffe-Brown, who took their orientation initially
from periods of close immediate observation of single societal
complexes: in Malinowski's case, the Trobriand Islanders of Papua
New Guinea, and in Radcliffe-Brown's the Andaman Islanders
of the Indian Ocean. This concentration on the ethnography of
a particular people as the stimulus and foundation for theorizing
and generalization set the tone for what became the predominant
pattern in ethnographic writing throughout much of the twentieth
century. Value was placed on in-depth understanding, the learning
of a local language and participant observation based on taking part
in local activities in the field. Such a shared ethnographic method,
however, did not in itself produce a uniformity of theory. (Frazer, by
the way, himself saw the value of Malinowski's in-depth 'scientific'
fieldwork.)

Malinowski, in his theorizing mode, attempted a holistic and
layered approach, building up his picture from biological needs
to technical means of satisfying these, to the social and cultural
integrative underpinnings that he saw as necessary to support viable
life patterns. Radcliffe-Brown adopted a narrower, but more focused
approach, in which he concentrated on the putative social functions

of practices in creating or maintaining group solidarity. There is no necessary opposition between these approaches, since both are ultimately functionalist and concerned with the reproduction of social patterns by cultural means. There is no doubt, however, that Malinowski was more interested in individuals and their psychological dispositions and motivations; while Radcliffe-Brown was more concerned with the moral upholding of social norms by role-bearing persons in society. It is quite likely that this difference was in part due to different field experiences. Malinowski's fieldwork was longer and more intense among the Trobrianders; Radcliffe-Brown perhaps did not come so personally close to his informants among the Andaman Islanders, although his work does show a detailed and deep understanding of them.

Both of these authors dealt with complex cycles of communal rituals, embracing the life cycle and the seasonal cycles of production and harvest in the case of the Trobrianders. Malinowski's ideas on Trobriander magic became particularly well known in theoretical discussions. The contexts range from garden magic to fishing in dangerous waters to spells to persuade reluctant exchange partners to hand over valuables in the inter-island ceremonial exchanges known as *kula* (Malinowski, 1922, 1935).

The garden-magic context is classic for understanding how Trobriand magical rituals worked. First, the power of magic was linked to the ancestors, a point which negates Frazer's rigid distinction between the domains of magic and religion. Second, magic was in the hands of a specialist, the *towosi*, linked by kinship to a ranked chief in the community. The *towosi* not only made magic, he also organized the actual work of clearing the garden ground, starting with sacrificial offerings of fish to the ancestral spirits. He and his helpers searched for magic bush herbs to bind onto the workers' axes. After the spirits' blessing was asked for, the *towosi* pronounced spells (*yopa*), the most important being the *vatuvi* spell calling on named ancestors to lead the way and imaging the garden as growing like a child in the mother's womb, as well as 'sweeping away' all troublesome insects and pests. The workers decorated themselves and proceeded ritually to the garden area, where the magician performed more spells and struck the soil with his magic wand to impart fertility to it. Then the men buckled down to the work of clearing the garden with their axes which were strengthened by the magic substance packets applied to them. Productive work and ritual were indissolubly bound together (see ch. 19 in Stewart and Strathern, 2010, pp. 311–21).

Trobriand gardens required hard work and knowledge to make them grow well, consisting of pockets of soil in coral. Magic added incentive and certainty to the task. Similarly, in open-sea fishing where the waters were turbulent beyond the lagoon and its outer coral reef, fishermen used magic to enhance their prospects of success. And in *kula* expeditions, when men travelled by canoe to other islands and asked for valuables in the circuits of exchange, they would beautify themselves with decorations and magic spells so as to dazzle their partners and overcome the latters' reluctance to part with their wealth goods (see also Kuehling, 2005, p. 150, pp. 198–99 on comparable practices on Dobu Island south of the Trobriands). All of these contexts are ones of risk and danger either of failure in one's aims or indeed loss of life at sea.

Stanley Tambiah (1968, reprinted in Stewart and Strathern eds, 2010, pp. 323–44) produced a detailed breakdown and concordance of all the specific ritual elements involved in Trobriand garden magic. He seeks to avoid a Frazerian interpretation in terms of sympathetic and contagious magical ideas, although it is clear that these ideas actually were at work. However, the important points that emerge from his discussion belong to what we would nowadays call practice theory. In particular, he seeks to understand the magic as a performative act and he decides that 'the technique [employed by the magician] gains its realism by clothing a metaphorical procedure in the operational or manipulative mode of practical action; it unites both concept and action, word and deed' (1968, p. 194, reprinted version p. 332). Tambiah also provided an eloquent exposition of the intimate symbiosis between what we might separate as magical and technical activity. In truth, it is probably an ethnocentric mistake to separate these categories at all, and Tambiah adduces another dimension of analysis which today we would label as embodiment theory. He notes the magic of abstinence applied to the yam storage houses filled at harvest-time and remarks that for Trobrianders the belly is the seat of emotions and memory (p. 201, p. 339). The expression of the magician regarding 'the belly of my garden' thus gains its true force. When Tambiah speaks of the conjoining of words and actions, we may go further and say that the words are in fact actions themselves, and the whole combination of activities of the magic constitutes its perceived ritual efficacy.

Radcliffe-Brown paid homage to the work of Frazer, if briefly, at the beginning of one of his papers, on Taboo, delivered as the Frazer lecture for 1939. He spoke of Frazer 'as an example of life-long single-minded devotion to scientific investigation' (1965, p. 133; first published in 1952). In this regard, he was at one with Frazer in viewing anthropology's task as the work of establishing a science of human society and culture. However, he set aside, by and large, the evolutionary component of such a science and saw social anthropology as an enterprise concerned ultimately with nomothetic studies in which acceptable generalizations were developed (1965 [1952], p. 3). He famously contrasted such an aim with the aims of historical enquiry, which he saw as idiographic and particular in scope. He did recognize that some historical studies could also be sociological and nomothetic in aim, mentioning the work of Fustel de Coulanges (on lineage structures and religion in the ancient cities of Greece and Rome) as an example (p. 2, see Coulanges n.d.). It is also of some interest to note that, as he himself records, he went into the field among the Andamanese with the aim of making a hypothetical account of the history of the Andamans and other Negrito populations in the Malayan Peninsula and the Philippines (Radcliffe-Brown 1964, relating to 1908–09 when he wrote the first version of his book). He decided, however, that the approach had limited value owing to lack of data, and he turned to the contemporary contexts of customary life.

In the 'Andaman Islanders' book, after reviewing earlier psychological theories that suggested religion began with propositions about dreams and reflections or with feelings of awe in the presence of nature, Radcliffe-Brown formulated his theory of sentiments, making these central to the workings of relationships in society (1964, pp. 233–34). He argued that such sentiments were inculcated through periodically conducted ceremonies (ibid.). Finally, he proposed that 'the social function of the ceremonial customs of the Andaman Islanders is to maintain and transmit from one generation to another the emotional dispositions on which the society (as it is constituted) depends for its existence' (p. 234). He recognized here the importance of the people's own explanations of their customs (p. 235) as clues to their analysis although not the underlying reasons for the customs. In pursuing his own interpretations he further assumed 'that when the same or a similar custom is practiced on different occasions it has the same or a similar meaning in all of them' (p. 235).

He proceeded to his examples, giving as the first the Andamanese marriage ceremony in which the couple are required publicly to embrace, culminating with the groom sitting on the bride's lap, expressing their sexual union as a fact witnessed by the community and therefore cemented and validated. Although he eschews comparisons, the similarity to the customs of his own culture are obvious here, including a reference to the practice of making gifts to the new couple. His second example is the North Andamans peacemaking ceremony, which he describes earlier in the book (pp. 133–35). He first notes that a man who has killed someone of another village goes into seclusion in the forest, observes taboos, and undergoes purification by being rubbed with white clay and red ocher paint: all this to avoid a revenge attack by the spirit of the man he killed. Later, at the peace ritual the previously hostile parties meet in the territory of the ones who made the most recent attack. Women are instrumental in arranging the meeting, and at it they sit on one side of the ground, while their men sit in front of a decorated cane stretched across the dancing area. The hosts do not carry weapons, but the visitors customarily do. They dance in and out of the row of male hosts, making threatening shouts and finally shaking each of the hosts. The women visitors then do the same. 'When the women have been through their dance the two parties of men and women sit down and weep together' (p. 135). The actions here correspond to a drama that begins with an epideictic display of ritualized aggression, in which the visitors have the license to threaten and the hosts must remain still, allowing the visitors' anger to subside, so that the two sides can be reconciled. No wealth goods appear to have been exchanged but Radcliffe-Brown particularly notes the action of weeping together, which we may interpret as the re-establishment of mutuality and empathy after a rupture.

Radcliffe-Brown also recognizes these ritual acts as a performance. He notes (p. 239) that ritual weeping is not spontaneous: 'it is always a rite the proper performance of which is demanded by custom' (ibid.). He surveys a range of contexts in which such a ritual of weeping is observed. When friends or relatives meet after being apart for some time they embrace and weep; ex-enemies embrace and weep in the peacemaking ritual; friends of mourners for a death weep with them at the conclusions of the mourning period as well as weeping over the boy; relatives of a couple weep over them at their marriage; and during initiation rituals the female relatives of initiands weep over them. In general, Radcliffe-Brown argues, these acts all reaffirm social bonds. They also recognize tension, and the weeping is a way of overcoming this tension, he says (p. 241).

He also acknowledges that senses of loss or transformation in relationships lie at the heart of acts of weeping, as when a mother weeps at her child's marriage because the child will now be partly separated from her. In all of these rites, he suggests, 'the purpose of the rite is to bring about a new state of the affective dispositions that regulate the conduct of persons to one another' (p. 245).

Several things are notable here. It is quite evident that Radcliffe-Brown was in fact interested in affect, as it contributed to social functions. Second, the interpretations he gives are his own. He does not cite the views of the Andamanese themselves. He does, in a sense, appeal to transcultural features of acts such as embracing or weeping. Andamanese society was relatively egalitarian, fragmented, and small-scale, and the groups had been greatly disturbed by processes of contact with the outside world and internal conflicts, so the kinds of functions of solidarity he was talking about were highly significant. His remarks seem reasonable and modest and closely tied to the empirical data he presents. All this is a far cry from the sort of narrow concept of function often attributed to Radcliffe-Brown. He does apply the same basic ideas, however, in his comparative writings, as when, for example, he reviews Emile Durkheim's theory of religion and the sacred. He agrees with Durkheim's idea 'that the primary object of the ritual attitude is the social order itself'; but he adds (Radcliffe-Brown, 1965, p. 124) that we have to ask what the relationship to the social order is that is expressed in such ritual attitudes to objects. Basically, he says, the object stands for the sentiment of 'attachment to the group' (ibid.). But why are natural objects and creatures so often chosen for this purpose, he asks.

He answers that, especially among hunting and gathering peoples (such as the Andamanese), there are ritual attitudes to all manner of animals and plants that are ecologically important. He mentions further a parallel between, for example, attitudes to the turtle among the Andamanese and attitudes to saints in the Roman Catholic religion – based on different cosmological ideas that associate or differentiate nature and culture. Totemism, as a variety of religious practice establishes, he says, 'a system of social solidarities' between people and the natural world (p. 131). The subtlety and care with which Radcliffe-Brown discusses these issues indicates that his work should not be dismissed as simply outdated structural-functionalism or unconcerned with wider issues of generalization (an observation that must modify the critiques mounted by I. C. Jarvie in 'The Revolution in Anthropology' in 1964). In other words, Radcliffe-Brown's pioneering work in intensive fieldwork was complemented by his insistence on a comparative approach; and his interests in social functions of practices proceeded through, rather than neglecting, questions of meaning (see, e.g. his discussions of meanings in his chapter on 'Taboo', pp. 133–52 in Radcliffe-Brown, 1965; also Moore, 2012, pp. 134–45, especially p. 144, where he suggests that 'the ideas of Radcliffe-Brown may deserve open-minded re-reading').

Jerry Moore, in the work mentioned above, remarks that Radcliffe-Brown was disliked by the students of Franz Boas in America. He nevertheless influenced others, such as Fred Eggan and Sol Tax who passed on that influence to their students (e.g. Keith Brown, who was influential in rethinking the character of the *dozoku* descent group in Japan and in promoting long-term fieldwork).

Boas's work and vision of anthropology was foundational for what became known as American cultural anthropology as opposed to British social anthropology. There is both institutional truth and philosophical inaccuracy in this historical dichotomy. As we have seen, Radcliffe-Brown's approach linked culture and social structure together. Thus, culture, however defined, was not left out of his scheme. Boas, nevertheless, stressed the importance of culture and of studying it in order to understand the viewpoints of the people studied, as a prime objective of ethnographic research. His definition of culture was also very inclusive and wide ranging. In these regards, Boas's perspectives resemble those of his fellow-European, Bronislaw

Malinowski, more than those of Radcliffe-Brown; and the holism that he espoused in ethnographic terms became subsequently the basis of the now time-honoured if contested paradigm of four-field anthropology – cultural, physical, archaeological and linguistic.

Here we are concerned with a central ritual practice of the Kwakiutl, the potlatch. This institution attracted a great deal of attention from scholars in economic anthropology because of the destruction of items of value that constituted a part of it, raising the question of the purposes and meaning that underlay the institution. Boas carried out intensive fieldwork in the Kwakiutl area with successive visits overtime, and also maintained a long correspondence with a major informant and collaborator, George Hunt (Codere, 1966, p. xxxi). The Kwakiutl people lived on and around Vancouver Island on the coast of British Columbia. Boas's work with them began around the same time as the Cambridge University Torres Straits expeditions to British New Guinea of 1888 and 1898. He insisted on the study of the local languages and the collection of materials in them as the proper basis for knowledge of the Kwakiutl and others around them: an insistence that fed into the creation of the four-field approach in American academic anthropology and remains the foundation of ethnographic fieldwork principles.

The Kwakiutl lived in villages, subdivided into *numayma* groupings, meaning 'one kind' (Boas, 1966, p. 37). Each village constituted a separate 'tribe', identified by their locality. The ancestor of each *numayma* 'appeared at a specific locality by coming down from the sky, out of the sea, or from underground, generally in the form of an animal, took off his animal mask, and became a person' (Boas, 1966, p. 42). Tribes were formed out of amalgamations of unrelated *numayma* that came together for defence, and each *numayma* occupied its own section of the village. Kin terms did not distinguish between maternal and paternal ties, but most marriages were made outside of the *numayma*.

Within the *numayma*, structure was provided not simply by genealogy, but by positions of defined rank, described as 'seats' or 'standing places' in the language (Boas, 1966, p. 50). Individuals occupied these seats at different times, and might do so in more than one *numayma* to which they had kin ties, taking as their names the titles of the seats themselves. Each *numayma* also had a head chief, a male whose wife held the title of 'Lifting the Dress in the House', from the ceremonial garb she wore in giving feasts.

Boas goes on to succinctly describe how status was obtained by making advantageous and appropriate marriage, by accumulating wealth 'by industry and by loaning out property at interest' (p. 51), and by disbursing that wealth ritually, 'with the understanding that each recipient of a gift has to return it with interest' later (ibid.). Boas explains that these acts of giving for returns were 'the general principle underlying the potlatch', a word he says came from the Nootka language (on the west coast of Vancouver Island).

Names, and their associated rank, could be obtained by inheritance and primogeniture, through either male or female lines. A firstborn daughter, then, took the family title. In general, numayma membership could be obtained through any line of descent (an arrangement we can variously call bilateral, cognatic or omnilineal). However, there was some gendered bias in favour of males, because women could not hold some ceremonial titles, and a daughter who succeeded to a title was given a male name and transmitted it to her eldest son (p. 52). In fact the head chiefs' names were said to have descended by primogeniture from their mythical ancestors.

Marriage was ideally between a couple of equal rank in different numayma, and was accompanied by an exchange of comparable wealth items, including blankets given by the groom's side and household goods from the bride's side, the latter exceeding the value of the bride price in blankets (p. 54). A valuable beaten copper might be given, along with a ranked name, by the bride's father to his son-in-law. Children who were born might continue to receive names from their mother's father. Boas noted that fictitious marriages might be entered into, with the primary aim of transferring names. Boas describes the marriage arrangements as integral with potlatch gifting. Announcements of the names of persons to whom gifts were distributed were an important part of the proceedings.

Names were acquired in sequence after a child's birth, and the elders of the group helped the child to distribute gifts in order to validate these acquisitions. Relatives of chiefly rank were particularly supposed to help (p. 77). The items used were blankets. Helen Codere explains that in Boas's time these were trade blankets, obtained for 50 cents each from the Hudson's Bay trading company, although 'in pre-contact times there had been blankets of cedar bark or various kinds of fur sewn together' (Codere, 1950, pp. 63–64). These blankets were loaned out for interest. When a boy took his third name, he would have to repay his creditors with 100 per cent interest if a year or more had passed since he received the loan (Boas, 1966, p. 79). Later, he could take part in potlatching proper, succeeding to his own father's seat or name by giving away large numbers of blankets and holding a feast.

Agonistic gifts were also made. Whole groups competed for rank as well as individuals. The recipient of a large number of blankets was said to be 'flattened' by them (Boas, p. 81). He could not refuse the gift, and was obliged to repay with 100 per cent interest. In another variety of potlatch the donor gave a large number of blankets and the recipient had to place 'an equal number of blankets on top of' these, prior to receiving the whole pile and becoming obliged to repay the whole total later (ibid.). Beaten coppers were items of high value, and could represent a large number of blankets. Purchase of a copper was accompanied by numerous 'financing' arrangements, and after the purchase the seller distributed the blankets paid for it to his creditors, adding new gifts if possible. The distribution was called 'doing a great thing' (p. 85). The sale of a copper was done between rival chiefs, and was accompanied by a large feast and elaborate speeches asserting rank and achievements through their acquired names. The feasting phases could also be agonistic. Food given at feasts to a chief had to be repaid. At a 'grease feast' huge quantities of candlefish (oulachon) oil might be poured out and burnt, requiring repayment. A chief might break up a copper and give the parts to a rival, who might then break one of his own and return both to the owner, or in a more flamboyant gesture might throw both broken coppers into the sea (p. 94). Songs asserted the greatness of the rival in these destructive contests, and one theme of praise was that the chief could boast that he was the only one who could make 'thick smoke rise' (p. 97) at feasts all the year round. Feast givers sometimes wore masks expressing their fierce qualities.

The Kwakiutl seem to have sought out a reputation for themselves as fierce warriors. In actual fact, only some men were trained as special warriors for a chief, used to make canoe voyages and sneak raids on victims. These attacks were often made on external enemies such as the Bella Coola, and were designed to kill people to make 'pillows' for dead relatives. Such killings cannot really be called revenge killings, since the attacks did not need to be made on relatives of those who had killed one's kinsman. Warfare was accompanied by the taking of heads and cannibalistic feats. Codere, quoting from an 1866 source (Lord) writes that 'heads were taken and tied to tall poles in front of the villages of the victors . . . .' (Codere, 1950, p. 107). Some wars were fought to obtain the crest and marks of status of the victims (Codere, p. 108). Warriors went into ecstatic states after killing others. At the great winter dance ceremonials bloodthirsty songs were sung extolling the feared exploits of warriors (Codere, p. 110). Some of these songs were themselves obtained through killing their former owners. Dances, too, might be obtained in this way. Codere emphasizes that the aim of appearing fierce in the winter dances outstripped the actual performance of violence in fighting.

We come now to a theme that links to the Papua New Guinea Highlands and the notion that gift exchange can substitute for fighting, or is itself a form of fighting. Gift-giving might then be seen as a sort of deflected or ritualized aggression. Clearly the idioms used by givers in the potlatch expressed directly the aim of defeating a rival and eclipsing his name. Looking at the matter historically, Boas quoted a speech in which it was said that 'in olden times we fought so that the blood ran over the ground. Now we fight with . . . blankets . . . and we smile at each other! Oh, how good is the new time!' (Boas, 1966, p. 119).

Codere discusses this viewpoint in detail in the last part of her work 'Fighting with Property' (which Michael Young echoed in his 'Fighting with Food', Young, 1971). She argues that the continuing motivation in Kwakiutl life was the unending pursuit of prestige, and that success in warfare and head hunting was over time replaced by success in potlatching (Codere, 1950, p. 118). That the change was precipitated by external control is suggested by a quote from a speech, to effect that 'The white man came and stopped up that stream of blood with wealth. Now we are fighting with our wealth' (Codere, p. 119). Blankets given away, as noted already, were said to flatten their recipients. Coppers might be called 'Means of Strife'. When broken they were said to be dead. Gifts were said to have the power to kill (i.e. overcome the recipient). Codere adduces stories from the mid-nineteenth century that variously indicate how stories of past killings might be woven into potlatch speeches; how two friendly chiefs might get into escalating competition over potlatching until one was driven into fighting in order to recover prestige; and how desires to possess a large copper might lead to killings. Codere notes that reports of the potlatch itself peter out after 1930, that the winter dances were last held in 1895, and that the last war happened in 1865. In addition she reports that introduced diseases had caused rapid population decline from 1837–1924, but that the remaining population had vigorously entered into trade with European incomers; and she reports European reprisals taken against the Kwakiutl for killing a war captive (taken as a slave, probably) around 1860. Finally, she suggests that 'as violence became increasingly ceremonialized and dramatized, instances of violence decreased in number' (p. 128).

There are some intriguing parallels with, but also divergences from, the histories of warfare, pacification, and the proliferation of exchange practices in the Mount Hagen area of the Western Highlands of Papua New Guinea since the 1930s. The parallels are as follows: In Mount Hagen, outsiders brought in large numbers of a type of valuable already culturally important, shell valuables, greatly increasing their availability as well as halting warfare by colonial control. Leaders seized on this opportunity to expand what are called *moka* exchanges and increase their prestige. The *moka* is based on a principle of increment like the potlatch, since items given in a *moka* have to be repaid with a greater number later. Speeches made at *moka* occasions claim prestige for both individual givers and their groups and recapitulate histories of past killings now set to rights with the gifts. *Moka* actions are replete with metaphors of conflict and killing: a gift may be said to be like a spear that dislodges the wig of a recipient (i.e. shames him by its size). And *moka* gifts must be repaid, on pain of losing prestige. Prestige is the final aim of social activity in the *moka*, and is described as making the 'name' of the *moka* giver 'go up' (Strathern, 2007).

Differences between *moka* and potlatch are no less striking. The first difference is the most important, and sheds some light on both sides of the ethnographies. In *moka* there is a clear historical transformation from compensation and reparation payments made to avert violence over killings into the metaphorical conflict (but also alliance-making) of *moka*. This clear process is lacking in the Kwakiutl case, for two reasons. First, among the Kwakiutl vengeance was not direct but might be transferred onto any victim; and second, indemnities were rarely paid by wealth (though sometimes a slave might be killed as a death for a death). These two structural features set the Kwakiutl apart from the Hageners. Crucially, also, in Hagen there was (and is) no equivalent of the Kwakiutl system of ranked names as titles or seats belonging to individuals and groups. There is only a generalized competition between leaders for 'name' or prestige as a fluid social process. Hagen society is based on achievement through exchange and the groups that support leaders in exchange, but the contest does not have the specific fierceness of the Kwakiutl case. In both cases (Kwakiutl and Hagen) it appears that there has been a historical shift from warfare to exchange via pacification, and correspondingly to the adoption of the symbolism of warfare into the world of exchanges. Finally, however, in Hagen there was no specialized category of warriors, nor was there any special value given to cruelty. Warriors were not segregated from society at large, but integrated into it, and values associated with exchange appear never to have been subordinated to those of violence. The complex inter-segmentary character of Hagen politics also maintained a wider arena of security via marriage alliances than appears to have held for the Kwakiutl. In terms of ritual theory, the values associated with peacemaking by compensation and prestige-making through *moka* have proved more enduring than the values of agonistic gifting did among the Kwakiutl. Hageners also directly incorporated money into their *moka* from the 1960s onward, thus making a bridge between the commodity-based new transactions they entered into with cash cropping and the values associated with the earlier exchanges of shells (Strathern and Stewart, 2000). They also had, and have, an indigenous valuable of great ritual significance, their pigs, and these remain central in *moka* exchanges or their latter-day equivalents in large-scale compensation payments for more recent deaths that are still made today.

An overall conclusion that we can draw here is that ritual practices can become the sites of cultural transformation and creativity in difficult historical changes. We will carry this point further in the next chapter, looking at the work of Victor Turner on rituals as forms of healing and conflict settlement.

4

Structure and process:
Victor Turner

Victor Turner's work built on the structural-functional model of
society but took into account historical change, processes of
conflict, the significant work of individual ritual specialists, and the
element of drama in ritual. As well, he identified different levels of
meanings in ritual activities. For Turner, structure was always turning
into process, with the possibility of change. Turner is well known also
for his elaboration of the idea of the 'liminal' and 'communitas', both
developed out of Van Gennep's original model of stages in initiation
rites (Turner, 1969, *The Ritual Process*).

A concomitant of the turn towards intensive fieldwork observations
in anthropology was the fact that 'the field' became in some ways the
touchstone of broader theorizing or the source of ideas and schemes
of thought that anthropologists developed, perhaps long after the
initial field experience was completed. In Victor Turner's case, he
and his wife Edith Turner went into the field with the Ndembu people
of Northern Rhodesia (since Zambia) while Turner was among a
number of researchers at the Rhodes-Livingstone Institute where
Max Gluckman was the Director (following Godfrey Wilson). The
Ndembu are a congeries of people who historically belonged to
the larger Lunda empire of Mwantiyanva and migrated southwards,
incorporating smaller indigenous groups into themselves (Turner,
1996 [1957], p. 14). The empire was involved in slave-trading, and
the Ndembu headmen also kept slaves in their household retinues,

transacted in payments of debts, fines, or homicide compensation and obtained unusually as children, sometimes sister's children within the matrilineage (Turner, 1996, p. 189). In other regards Ndembu society was relatively egalitarian, villages were small, and people often moved from place to place.

The principal structural features of Ndembu social networks were marital virilocality combined with matrilineal descent. That is, wives were expected to join their husband's village (= virilocal marriage) but their children belonged to their own natal maternal lineage where their mothers came from (= matrilineal descent). This combination of rules made for a structural contradiction at the heart of village continuity. Village leaders tried to keep both their own children and those of their sisters. Leaders also tried to practice polygyny, leading to conflict between the children of separate wives and to the tendency of uterine sibling groups to hive off from others in a village and found their own settlements. Descent and locality pulled in opposite directions, and the growth of large groups or matrilineages with deep genealogies was inhibited. Subsistence practices of growing cassava and finger-millet enabled groups to move easily, and there was, besides, a great emphasis on male practices of hunting for game in forests, which was counterposed to matrilineal descent and the combined female and male labour that went into gardening. The fissile characteristics of Ndembu kinship relations are indicated clearly in Turner's statement that 'men and women own their own gardens and spouses have no rights in one another's gardens' (Turner, 1996, p. 23). Turner's detailed descriptions emphasize residential mobility rather than stability; but in a deeper analysis he points out that 'The men are present and together because of dead women; the women are absent because they are married to other men' (p. 60). These features were highly significant for influencing patterns of ritual practices. Villages were fissile and potentially divided units, while a widespread membrane of ties of kinship and affinity linked people together across villages. These links too could be broken by divorce, but a special honorific term used between a man and his ex-spouse's husband ensured that he could visit any children of his from the former marriage. Turner moves on to consider how rituals played a part in resolving the innumerable conflicts that arose in communities divided in this way.

Rituals tying people together, in spite of the divisive pulls inherent in the contradiction between matrilineal descent and virilocal marriage, were life-crisis rituals and 'cults of affliction' (Turner, 1996 [1957], p. 292). Because of the dispersed character of kin ties life-crisis events brought together categories of people from different places. Cults of affliction did the same, centring on persons who were said to have been 'caught' for forgetting to make small oblations to their ancestors, or for quarrelling with their living kin. 'Caught' here means that a man involved in this way will suffer bad luck at hunting and a woman will suffer reproductive disorders (p. 292). The afflicting spirit would be a deceased relative. A woman, for example, might dream that such a relative appeared to her as a hunter, with a symbolic red feather in her hair, and red things would be deployed to cure her (red clay, red tree-gum, blood). The curing ritual meant her entry into a curative cult, and it was carried out by adepts who themselves had been previously cured (p. 293), or if they were male had assisted in the curing of their sister or wife. The adepts gained status over time by taking part in the curing rituals for others, and they would participate in such rituals anywhere among the Ndembu. Curing sequences were social occasions, accompanied by dancing, singing and beer drinking, bringing prestige to the village headman. Meanwhile the adepts and their patient would retire in secrecy to the bush, ending their treatment with a sacrifice of a chicken or a goat to appease the offended spirit. The kinship connections of the patient with this spirit were recapitulated and divination was used to determine what had caused the offence in the first place. Sometimes matrilineal ties were renewed in this way. Because of the prevalence of this mode of ritual curing almost all villagers were adepts of one or other of four major curing societies concerned with women's reproduction. In addition, there were the men's societies concerned with hunting, which also linked people across groups; and new practices introduced from elsewhere to deal with misfortunes said to be caused by dead Europeans (p. 298), or as anti-witchcraft cults. Finally, the Ndembu practiced cross-community girls' and boys' initiations. Turner notes that all these rituals were performed quite frequently and that through them disputes and discontents were constantly being aired and settled (p. 301). Rituals bring the experience of suffering into the open, so that, Turner concludes, 'the affliction of each is the concern of all' (p. 302), and rituals knit together what was torn asunder by the contradictions inherent in the kinship field of relations.

Turner describes in detail an example of the Chihamba ritual, which involves the manifestation of a dangerous ancestor spirit that can kill people because of its pervasive anger against any slight that it imagines has been made against it. The spirit is supposed to speak in a rough way, or through the medium of Kavula, an old term for the power of lightning. An adept would play the part of Kavula in a ritual drama, asking questions of the initiates and giving them new names. The initiates, male and female, crawled towards a representation of Kavula, and each candidate was enjoined then to strike this representation and kill Kavula. A chicken was sacrificed and its blood said to be Kavula's. The candidates were declared in the ritual process to be Kavula's 'slaves' (p. 305). While Kavula was said to be male, the afflicting spirit was spoken of as female, and his wife, identified by divination (pp. 305–06). When the ordeals of the initiates were over, a special friendship was said to be created between the adepts and the candidates. In a detailed exposition, Turner identifies the socially healing effects of one such Chihamba ritual in Mukanza village (pp. 315–16), such as inducing sympathy for a senior woman in the village and reducing in-group factionalism.

These kinds of ethnographic accounts, meticulously documented, formed the core of Turner's subsequent highly elaborated explorations in wider kinds of analyses. He greatly developed Van Gennep's notion of the liminal stages that initiates undergo, which Turner describes as a sort of liminal 'no-man's-land' (Turner, 1985b, p. 295) in between a past and a future, within which the initiands experience remarkable dramas and may be tested in all kinds of ways. It was to this domain of experience that he referred when he wrote of culture in the 'subjunctive mood' (1985b), a time of fantasy and potentiality from which order may emerge. Turner in fact saw initiation rites as examples of a wider class of ritually played out social dramas. The complete form of these dramas he identified as: breach, crisis, redress, reintegration or schism. The social context of conflicts among the Ndembu seems to loom large in this formulation, but Turner means it to refer to a broader class of ritualized actions, in which he saw divination carried out to determine the causes of an illness or to provide prognostications for the future as an important instrument of redress and thus as a part of steps towards healing. He saw these liminal stages of rituals also as important for effecting changes, because they encapsulate formlessness or freedom from the constraints of everyday life. He noted that the artistic figures that are often created for initiation rites among the Ndembu could 'display a wide range of personal aesthetic initiative' (1985b, p. 160). And he went on to argue that liminal phases of action contain within them aspects of play, and further that play itself is 'a serious business' (p. 160): in other words that it can convey serious messages about social relationships in a kind of 'metalanguage' (p. 163) that enables discourse about social life to take place in collective contexts where 'multivocal' symbols are brought into relief, such as the famous *mudyi* tree among the Ndembu that exuded sap reminiscent of mother's milk and at a more abstract level of the matrilineal principle. Play as a concept here is very close both to the idea of the imagination as a force in cultural creativity and to the idea of metaphor in particular as an ingredient in the genesis of symbols. What we call metaphor is the process of translation of one meaning of a term into another realm. Typically, in English language contexts, what is thought of in other ways as an 'abstract' category or value, is expressed by the metaphor in 'concrete' terms, but this is not a necessary condition. (Note that 'concrete' here is itself a transposition of meaning akin to metaphor.) Metaphor is also like simile with an ellipsis, the distance between the referent and the image that conveys it being collapsed. For example, in the well-known expression from the love poem by Robert Burns, the object of the poet's love is said to be like 'a red, red rose that's newly sprung in June', giving an image of freshness and vividness that is drawn from the characteristics of the flower. He goes on to say that his love is also 'like a melody, that's sweetly sung in tune'. The first image appeals to the senses of vision and smell, the second to the harmonies of sound. Here the simile is preserved in the term 'like', but all the stress is on the (metaphorical) set of images themselves. The important symbols deployed by the Ndembu in their rituals might be seen as embodied metaphors, gaining their significance from the contexts of performances in which they were mobilized to carry out the work of the ritual itself. Turner himself used the term 'root paradigms' (1985b, p. 167) in this context.

Overall, Turner stressed that his approach to rituals, and social life generally, was processual. He applied this approach to the study of ritual symbols. For him such symbols tended to carry multiple significations or meanings – he referred to their multi-vocality or polysemy (1985b, p. 171) and he argued that these meanings can shift over time, be added to or subtracted from events and carry varying personal meanings for the performers of a ritual. As his ideas developed, Turner frequently revisited this classic question of the meanings of symbols. For example, he identified certain symbols, such as that of the *mudyi* tree mentioned above, as dominant in a ritual complex, noting that symbols of this kind have the properties of condensation of meanings, polarization into ideological and visceral or sensory elements, and the unification of disparate elements into a single complex (Turner, 1967, p. 28). In another treatment he distinguished between three levels of meanings of symbols: (1) exegetical meanings, those given by the people themselves (often in practice, it should be noted, by experts rather than others); (2) what he called the operational meanings, that is, how meanings are displayed in action, as perceived by the ethnographers; and finally (3) the positional meaning, that is, meanings as they appear in relation to another symbols in the total ritual – this, too, is established by the ethnographer, building on levels (1) and (2). Turner saw importance in noting the affective value given to symbols at the operational level, that is, in appreciating their emotive power for the participants, and this seems a vital point. Another interesting feature of Turner's treatment is his discussion of what the term 'symbol' would correspond to in the Ndembu people's own language. He writes that the term is *chinjikijilu* from *ku-jikijila*, 'to blaze a trail', by making marks on a tree or bending branches on a pathway. A symbol, therefore, shows a way that can be followed; as Turner puts it, a path from the known to the unknown (Turner, 1967, p. 48). A comparative study of indigenous terms like this would yield considerable insight both into people's world views and into questions of translation of those views into an abstract term like the word 'symbol' itself (see Turner, 1992, edited by Edith Turner).

Turner's later work broadened out into further domains of exploration. Aside from his work on pilgrimages (e.g. 1992, pp. 29–47), Turner turned his attentions to the study of performance as a category of analysis, to the anthropology of experience, and to the transformation of ritual into theatre via the concept of play and what he called its 'human seriousness' (Turner, 1982). As with all his work, the roots of his approaches to these topics lay in his original Ndembu fieldwork. The conflicts he observed there were ones he described as 'social dramas', both because of their patterned forms and because the participants in them were self-consciously aware of their being observed, that they were in fact performing for spectators in contexts of crises (1985b, p. 180), especially in what he calls the redressive phase of settling a conflict caused by an initial breach of norm. There are also, he notes, following work by Sally Falk Moore, creative and improvised attempts to overcome indeterminacy in social life. It is these attempts also that Turner calls performances (p. 185), and he suggests that these entail the performers coming to know themselves better. Performances include both verbal and non-verbal communication, and Turner identifies drama and theatre as prime exemplifications of performance. He insists that the essence of life and experience is that it is dynamic, like a quest for meaning, appealing to the philosopher Wilhelm Dilthey's concept of *Weltanschauung*, world view as expressed in lived experience. Turner also thought that major contemporary genres of cultural performance such as appear in theatre and film draw their force from the same 'social drama' concept that he found helpful in analyzing his Ndembu materials (p. 201). These views he set out further in his account of a 'new processual anthropology', utilizing again Dilthey's ideas, particularly his concept of the Erlebnis, defined and meaningful experience (1985b, p. 212) that combines cognition and affect together. He comes back in the end, via a series of etymological excursions, to the model of rites of passage, as journeys by which initiands gain knowledge through performances (trials, ordeals) – the same, indeed, for pilgrimages. Movement is intrinsic to all of these images and the metaphor of life as a journey and a path with a beginning and an end is the underlying principle here. Turner followed up his interests in the anthropology of experience in the volume he edited on the topic with Edward M. Bruner (Turner and Bruner eds, 1986). In this volume he meditates further on the importance of drama, and other contributors add elements to the definition of performance. For example, Bruce Kapferer argues that performance 'constitutes a unity of text and enactment' with a directionality or intention behind it (Kapferer in Turner, 1986, pp. 192–93). This fits well enough with Turner's own idea of the social drama, with its progression from breach of norm to the enactment of redress.

Finally, here, Turner brought his ideas about the social drama to further fruition in his book *From Ritual to Theatre* (1982). Here he introduces the concept of the liminoid as distinct from the classic liminal category that belongs to rites of passage. Liminal, or threshold, phases in rites of passage are ones in which the actors are suspended in a transitional phase and are thrown together also in an unstructured communitas or sense of shared experience prior to the re-establishment of a structured set of roles in a new configuration. Turner sees the place of ritual as a combination of work and play, developed in societies in which distinctions between work and leisure time are not marked. Thus ritual can be both work and play and play can be serious. With the advent of industrialization the distinction between work and leisure became more marked, he argues, and the liminal category became instead the 'liminoid', expressed in optional categories of activities that may be individual rather than collective (1982, p. 52). The liminoid thus takes the place of the liminal in some contexts of 'complex, modern societies', although the liminal category still exists in these also. Turner proceeds to theorize the category of the liminoid further, drawing on Mihaly Csikszentmihalyi's concept of 'flow' as a harmonious stream of action (p. 56) that is autotelic, does not need goals outside of itself (p. 58). However, flow in this sense does not have to be seen as peculiar to industrial societies or to liminoid contexts, nor need it be divorced from purposive activities beyond itself. Making an artifact or a garden is purposive, and the act of doing so may also constitute flow. Indeed, the same can be said of ritual activities.

Victor Turner's later work ranged over a very wide arena of topics, and is itself indicative of a seriously playful or inventive engagement with questions of creativity as well as of performance in ritual. One of his mature essays deals with a major classic topic in the study of ritual, that is the meanings of sacrifice as ritual action. Consistently with his overall approach, he sees sacrifice as a process within larger sequences of ritual action, and he goes to the Ndembu ethnography for his exposition. Quarrels and conflicts, that were endemic to

Ndembu society, were thought to offend the shades of ancestors, *akishi*, who might then send sickness to their living kin to warn them against carrying conflict too far and rendering themselves vulnerable to attacks by witches and sorcerers. Diviners were employed to discover which ancestors were involved and what the root causes were of quarrels as well as what rituals, including sacrifices, would be needed to cure people of their sicknesses. In major rituals the aim was not simply to alleviate the sickness of individuals but to transform enmities into amity by means of sacrifices. Turner details the performance of the Chihamba ritual involving the deity Kavula to demonstrate his point, and he equates the aim of producing amity or love both with his concept of communitas and with the idea of flow (1992, p. 104). 'Sacrifice', he adds, 'is one very important means of restoring the flow' (p. 105); and he adduces the ancient Roman ritual of *lustratio*, or procession to purify the earth, as a further example, calling the *lustratio* a 'frame-maintenance' rite (p. 108). Or, as he also puts it, sacrifice may be regarded as a limen, or entry into the domain of communitas (p. 110). Society itself, he suggests, in a phraseology reminiscent of Frazer, may have to die in order to be reborn (p. 112). In our next chapter we compare these imaginative insights with those of another anthropologist of African societies, Meyer Fortes.

5

Ancestor worship and sacrifice: Meyer Fortes, psychological interpretations and divination

Turner's work clearly dealt with emotions as well as social structure. Meyer Fortes also built a part of his work on the ambivalent emotional relations between fathers and firstborn sons, using his extensive fieldwork on the Tallensi people of Ghana as his source of analytical inspiration. Fortes emphasized filial piety in the Tallensi system and the ritual in which it was expressed as the means of controlling father-son hostility. Thus, the function of ritual as a means of controlling aggression came to the forefront in this work. One of the contexts involved was that of sacrifice (Fortes, *Oedipus and Job in West African Religion*, 1983). One of Fortes's enduring concerns was with the creation and maintenance of social order, but this does not mean that he saw such order as emerging automatically out of customary rules. He quite clearly recognized that struggles and conflicts occur at the heart of social relations, and that ideological and practical considerations are brought to bear in the effort to achieve order. While he did not use the term social drama that Turner later developed, the struggles he depicted among kinsfolk obviously do constitute such dramas in the broad sense that Turner gave to the term.

For inspiration and comparative insight into his extensive field materials on the Tallensi people of Ghana in West Africa originally gathered in 1934–37, Fortes later drew on suggestive parallels from Old Testament and ancient Greek sources, hence the title of his book referring to Oedipus and Job mentioned above. The comparison with Job rests on the problem of theodicy or justice and obedience to the commands of a deity that may involve suffering. The parallel with Oedipus is based more closely on the control of institutionally recognized antagonism between fathers and eldest sons in the Tallensi familial system of kinship relations. Fortes's exposition indicates that this antagonism was rooted in the fact that the eldest son was designated as the successor to the father, but could not fully enter into that succession until the father was dead and became an ancestor. The eldest son, accordingly, was obliged to observe careful taboos in relation to this father. For example, from an age of roughly five or six years old, the firstborn son could not eat out of the same dish as his father, although his younger siblings could. The sons were educated to be well aware of these prohibitions. The firstborn could not eat chicken, could not look into the father's granary, wear his cap or tunic, or use his hunting bows and arrows (Fortes, 1987, p. 223). These taboos held until the death of the father, at which time the father was ritually transformed into an ancestor, and the eldest son had the duty of initiating the ritual sequence of actions; and at its end the taboos he had observed in relation to the father were abrogated. For example, the father's tunic and cap were turned inside out and placed on the successor. The eldest (that is, firstborn) son could also now look into the father's granary because he had succeeded to its ownership.

The background to these taboos is the expectation of antagonism between father and firstborn son. When the son reaches his teens ('adolescence') he and the father are forbidden to meet each other face to face in the entrance way to the family compound (Fortes, 1987, p. 226). The explanation in terms of the tensions of succession was a conscious model of the Tallensi themselves. A father might point to his son while still small and say that the boy was 'only waiting for me to die so that he can take my place' (1987, p. 226).

The tensions centre on the firstborns simply because they mark the irreversible transition to parenthood in the lineage structure of the Tallensi, and they carry with them the idea that their personal Destiny or Yin will grow up to challenge the Destiny of the father, unleashing a struggle of wills between them (see the account in Strathern and Stewart, 2010a, pp. 83–84).

What, then, controlled this supposed animosity between firstborn son and father? The rules of sacrifice to ancestors came into operation here. The lineage ancestors, installed in domestic proximity in special shrines, were considered to watch over their descendants and to resent any wrongdoing within the family. To appease them in cases of misfortune or sickness, only the living head of the household could conduct the necessary sacrifices. As long as the father lived, therefore, his children, including the firstborn, had to depend on him for this ritual mediation with the ancestors, in the first place with the father's own dead father. Thus, 'the ancestors are only accessible through the parents' (1987, p. 222). Ancestors were thought of as the ultimate sources of both prosperity and misfortune, and the key to approaching them was held only by male household heads whose fathers were deceased.

The image of the son waiting for his father to die was rooted, then, in these very specific arrangements. Fortes argued that the ideology of filial piety was what controlled the tensions in the system from breaking out. Such piety, as with its Roman equivalent, was based on the putative power of the ancestors. Not only respect, but fear must have been involved in the relationship. The duty of piety was relatively straightforward. The firstborn must observe the proper taboos and must ask the father to make sacrifices on his behalf. Piety therefore consisted of forms of respect and dependency, channelled into ritual practices.

The effectiveness of an act of sacrifice to ancestors depended, for the Tallensi, as for many other peoples, on the application of divinatory procedures to determine which ancestor might be implicated and why, so as properly to direct the sacrifice. Specialist diviners were needed in order to carry out these procedures in a legitimate and observable manner. These were part-time male adepts (Fortes, 1987, p. 12), who through experiments and trials had made shrines as homes for a congeries of ancestors, and then approached these ancestors to help them find out the causes of trouble for their consulting clients. The male bias here was increased by the rule that women could not independently consult a diviner. They had to go through their male relatives. Most divination was in fact negotiated through household heads as the immediate consultants. Diviners used a rattle, a strong stick, and a bag filled with code objects. The client approached by offering a small fee in advance, placing it in front of the diviner. The diviner would then clap the bag with his hands and quietly call on his ancestors to come and be present, seated on the divining shrine. The diviner shook his rattle and chanted the call to the ancestors, then took a pair of stones and threw them to the ground after spitting on them. One wet, one dry surface coming up meant that the ancestors accepted to participate further. The diviner then used his stick to sweep among the code objects from the bag until a selection emerged as chosen by the stick and from these further inferences were made. Fortes provides a list of objects and their standardized meanings for divination, for example, a fragment of a water tortoise's shell means coolness, or peace of heart. A diviner might use 20 or 30 such pieces to select from. When the 'answers' were obtained from the ancestors, a sacrifice would be instituted (Fortes, 1987, p. 20). These sacrifices could include libations of millet beer, or livestock such as fowls, sheep, goats, or for major occasions a cow.

Fortes's account of divination and sacrifice is set clearly into the framework of his exposition of Tallensi kinship relations and the emphasis on agnatic ties traced through senior males. Interestingly, he points out that whereas patrilineal ancestors were seen as custodians of debts and promises of material transactions, among people and in relation to themselves as ancestors, maternal ancestors were particularly feared as potentially minatory and punitive. Such ancestors have ramifying connections across patrilineal groups, and because of their potential for hostility it is thought wise to try to befriend them and turn them into helpers or divination monitors, as it were, he notes (Fortes, 1987, p. 13).

Fortes's account makes it very clear how sacrifices were an important part of problem-solving in life and in particular of dealing with sicknesses that were seen to be triggered by ancestral displeasure. In turn, divination in general is also an essential part of problem-solving because people see it as the only way, or one important way, of communicating with the hidden (occult) world of the spirits and finding out what they require by way of enabling a sick person to regain well-being. As Fortes so effectively stressed, the point here is not simply that a personalistic explanation of sickness is given, but also that a moral dimension enters in. Sickness is interpreted as a sign that something wrong has been done, and in order for the sick person to be healed, this wrong has to be put right (see, e.g. Fortes, 1987, pp. 102, 105). This requires that an authoritative diagnosis and prescription of appropriate action is required. Divination is the moment between diagnosis and therapeutics, as Winkelman and Peek put it (2004, p. 3). It also links the patient to a wider meaningful cosmos, and has the potential to reintegrate the community around the process of healing the sick person. Sickness is the pivot of this whole ritual process because it indicates that there is trouble in social relations as well as in the body of the one who is ill (in effect constituting what Turner called the social drama). The involvement of spirit beings is further an essential postulate of all divinatory work by specialists, amounting to a denial of chance or pure contingency in events and an attribution of causative meanings located in the relations between spirits and living humans. Particular local calculations of logic are made in order to establish such meanings. For the Tallensi we have seen how recognized 'code objects' were employed as logico-semantic operators in order to arrive at a diagnosis, using the 'real' character of these as a means of reaching out to the intangible world of the ancestors. Every divinatory system works in an analogous or parallel way to this Tallensi example. Writing on the Sukuma people of northwest Tanzania, Stroeken comments that these people practice two types of divination: one through an altered state of consciousness on the part of a medium, the other through a sacrifice of chickens by the diviner and the consultant (Stroeken, 2004, pp. 29–30). Both methods, Sukuma say, depend on the helping presence of ancestors. Mention of the chicken oracle may remind us of the classic case of Zande divination for witchcraft reported on by Evans-Pritchard (Evans-Pritchard, 1937, p. 42, quoted in Stewart and Strathern, 2004, pp. 65–66). In the Zande example, divination and sacrifice and therapy were all combined, since the chicken was thought to point to the identity of a witch causing someone to be sick as a result of being in effect sacrificed to the poison oracle, and its wing was then taken and presented to the person identified as the witch, with an invitation to blow out water on the wing and thus cool (remove) the witchcraft. For the Sukuma, Stroeken notes that people say that 'the chicken lives in the twilight of the homestead, perceiving what humans cannot' (Stroeken, 2004, p. 33). Stroeken argues that chickens and diviners share the characteristic of liminality (p. 33), and indeed one would expect that if divination entails border crossing into the spirit world, the diviner (or medium, or shaman) must indeed be seen as a liminal figure and the process of healing is thus like a rite of passage. Sukuma divination is itself an enactment of a passage of inspection inside the sacrificed chicken's body, in which the diviner, sickness and patient become like mirrors of one another. Parts of the chicken's insides are seen as marks of conditions of the patient's body; for example, if its gall bladder is full, this is interpreted as showing that the patient can still digest food (p. 39). The chicken's flesh also stands for the residential compound, its bone for the household, and its skin for the space occupied by the ancestors (p. 39). If witchcraft is suspected as the cause of an illness, the identity of the witch can be determined by the diviner inspecting the chicken's wing feathers (p. 43). The patient here is seen as situated on the joint of the chicken's wing, corresponding in social terms to the articulation of clan and neighbourhood ties (p. 44). Red marks on a feather can reveal the identity of the ancestor or the witch/sorcerer who has caused the illness. If a kinsperson is identified as the one who has made witchcraft or sorcery against the sick person as a victim, this is explained as because the person was 'ripe' for such vindictive action because they owed debts to their kin, who thereby gain a kind of right to 'eat' their life force. The witch is said to have an 'intrusive gaze' upon the victim, thus perhaps being viewed as like a privileged kinsperson who has nevertheless become distant or alienated from the victim as a result of enmity. The ways to combat the sickness include sacrifices 'on the ancestral altar within the compound' (p. 48), wearing of special protective amulets by the patient, and also the ingestion of herbal medicines. The therapy can be described as pluralistic. Stroeken refers to it as 'ecodelic', that is, letting the world or cosmos reveal itself to the sick person as their home or habitat in which order can be restored once the truth of the cause of sickness has been discovered via divination. This stress on the cosmos, and its instantiation in communal action, is also found in Edith Turner's reprise of Ndembu divinatory and healing practices in the same volume as Stroeken's study (E. Turner in Winkelman and Peek eds, 2004). Stroeken's detailed exposition of divination by chickens among the Sukuma offers a tantalizing possibility of explaining why the Azande also employed the wing of a divinatory chicken in therapy, asking the identified witch to make the witchcraft cool by blowing water onto the wing. For the Sukuma, too, making the wing cool or purified from the effects of sorcery/witchcraft was encompassed by dipping it in a bowl of water (Stroeken, p. 35). Again, for the Azande, blowing out water would entail mixing it with saliva – which is used as a means of identifying the consultant of an oracle among the Sukuma (Stroeken, p. 40). Stroeken's intimately observed and portrayed analysis, based equally on his anthropological perspective and on his own detailed training as a medium among the Sukuma, fits well also with what Martin Holbraad has arrived at in his discussion of Cuban divination: that what divination does is to transform the ontology of experience in patients and so provide them with a form of truth, which Holbraad describes as 'Truth in Motion', or truth revealed or created in the process of divinatory action itself. In this approach truth is performative, it emerges from the performance of the divination; and it is recursive, because it refers us back critically to what is meant by the concept of truth and contrasts the performative way it is defined in divination with the way it is purportedly defined in a Western philosophical epistemology (Holbraad, 2012). Holbraad's approach seems akin to that shared by the contributors to John Pemberton's edited volume on 'Insight and Artistry in African Divination' (Pemberton, 2000). The striking illustrations of objects and figures constituting the materials of oracular practice and divination in African contexts remind us forcibly of the artistic side of divination and of how art constructs its own forms of truth out of the material world (see, e.g. Plate 7, the Luba [Hemba] figure with a quartz insert on the top of the head said to signal the 'flash of the spirit' that emerges from a diviner entering into a state of possession, colour plates following p. 22, Pemberton, 2000. The worldwide significance of crystals as stores of power should be kept in mind while viewing this remarkable creation).

Holbraad's analytical stance may profitably be compared further to Don Handelman's concept of 'Ritual in its own Right' (Handelman and Lindquist eds, 2004); or to radical forms of phenomenology positing 'Things as they Are', as in the works of Michael Jackson (Jackson ed., 1996); or further with all analyses that take a hypothetical 'as if' form and then establish it as a kind of alterity in truth. At a very abstract level, it might also be compared with Jaques Derrida's idea that everything is a text ('il n'y a pas de hors de texte'). However, some caution would be needed at that point. Jesting Pilate may have asked 'what is truth?' and moved on without giving an answer; but the extreme relativism implied by a totally or indefinitely recursive idea of truth would lead us into fields of radical uncertainty in which all ethnographic work might founder. As long as we are within the imaginative worlds of the Cuban diviner, or the Sukuma medium, we can well understand both their logics and how these are activated in practice. But if we step outside of these worlds, where do we place our feet next? Holbraad, incidentally, takes inspiration from Roy Wagner's early work on the invention of culture and his study of the *habu* ritual among the Daribi people of Papua New Guinea, noting that Daribi ideas appear to invert 'Western' ones of nature and culture (Wagner, 1972, 1981), and that these kinds of inversions or reversals of perspective challenge the anthropologist's ways of conceptualizing culture itself as a leading concept in ethnography. It is an interesting point. However, we are dependent on Wagner's own ethnography for its starting place, that is on Wagner's account of how the Daribi think about their 'customs' (expounded by Holbraad, p. 40), including the *habu* curing ritual itself. In the *habu* the actors take on the characteristics of ghosts in order to enact a curing, and Wagner tells us that this act subverts a taken for granted distinction between the dead and the living. But this distinction itself may be a product of the anthropologist's own thought processes, similar to the ways in which some cognitive theorists regard religious ideas as 'counter-intuitive'. This subversion of conventional anthropological descriptions may thus itself be subject to being subverted. The valuable observation that is contained here is that ritual acts often do indeed have an imaginative, creative, aleatory and playful element in them, showing that they are improvisations, as Victor Turner powerfully argued long ago.

Seeing rituals, including those that involve sacrifice, as imaginative acts, helps us to understand how they may change or may take alternative forms in time and space. This was explained very clearly by different ritual experts who officiated in the Female Spirit rituals in the Mount Hagen area of Papua New Guinea during the 1960s–80s. When asked about their ways of setting up the sacred parts of the ritual site or their sacrificial spells, they would say that their ways of doing these things were particular to themselves and might well be different from those of other, rival experts – in other words, a recognition of individual variations, which might be the product of different micro-traditions or simply personal inventiveness (Strathern and Stewart, 1999).

We have reviewed theories of sacrifice in anthropology elsewhere (Strathern and Stewart, 2008a), looking particularly at what kinds of expectations of *exchange* sacrifices set up between people and spirits/deities and between people themselves. We drew on the classic account of Nuer sacrificial practices by Evans-Pritchard. To begin with, Evans-Pritchard, like many others, was drawn to the practices of blood sacrifices of animals in which the death of the animal was clearly offered to *Kwoth* (Spirit) with the intentions of ridding the community of sickness or pollution. The sacrifice is a *kok*, a means of obtaining a bargain with the deity in which the deity will feel obliged to be helpful, as a result of metaphorically 'eating' the life of the animal sacrificed. We can sense here a sort of improvisation of meanings as with the Daribi *habu*. Yet there is no doubt that this is all clearly in the sphere of 'custom' rather than pure 'invention', and the Nuer would certainly recognize this to be so. The use of extended meanings of 'eating' in contexts of sacrifice is shared between the Nuer and the Melpa speakers of Mount Hagen. In Hagen the spirits of the dead ancestors, to whom pigs might be dedicated in sacrifices, were spoken of as experiencing the rich aroma of the pork as it was cooked (much as the living do), and this act of smelling was also figured as a form of privileged consumption. They might be enjoined to 'eat' the sacrifice in this way rather than 'eating' the liver or other insides of a sick person. In general the ancestors were thought of as having a powerful hold over the fortunes of the living, so that if a man is trying to obtain shell valuables, say, from an external exchange partner he must enlist his ancestors' support to persuade the partner to let go of these wealth tokens, and so he must kill a pig in sacrifice.

The ancestors must always have their portion, and exchanges with both the living and the dead have to be kept straight. As we noted, if a man has promised to sacrifice a pig 'to his dead kin but then promises it to an exchange partner instead he will not succeed in his next quest . . . aligning words entails also aligning worlds of practice' (Strathern and Stewart, 2008a, p. xxiv). (For a direct parallel among the Tallensi, see Fortes, 1987, p. 16.)

Sacrifices of animals are generally expensive. Both Hageners and the Nuer acknowledge this fact.

There is clearly a political economy of sacrifice at work as well as an arrangement of social values around that economy. In Hagen what is at stake is the life, health and prosperity of people in a system of exchange in which pigs are a prime and enduring medium of value, and cannot easily be substituted with money, even though money can be used to obtain pigs themselves. The importance of the pig is iconically, or even indexically, linked to such values because pork contains *kopong* or 'grease' (fat, fertility, prosperity) equivalent to life and health. The sacrifice of a primary source of the very substance of life is therefore a suitable basis in terms of which a sick person's healthy life is restored to them. The political economy element enters in because pigs require a great deal of labour to raise, and this labour joins together the work of women and men in gardening and herding, so that people think carefully about alternative uses to which pigs can be put. As we have noted above, conflicts over the choices of what to do with pigs can have serious anticipated repercussions, and there may be a conflict between promises to ancestral kin and promises to living exchange partners. The ancestors may take precedence here because it is they who are instrumental, directly or indirectly, in sending sickness to their living kin. For Hageners, then, as for New Guinea Highlanders generally, there is traditionally no way of denying an obligation to sacrifice once this obligation has been established by acts of divination, and the ancestors always ask for pigs. In the act of sacrifice the pig must be killed, so that its full value has to be expended at that point, with, however, the bonus that the pork can be shared out and consumed by the living kin. The pig's whole exchange value as a living creature is thus liquidated, but its value as meat is divided out and shared and contributes further to an ongoing network of consumption and exchange.

With the Nuer, the equivalent of the pig was the ox, although animals such as goats or sheep could be employed (Evans-Pritchard, 1956, pp. 57–58, where elaborate specific protocols of sacrifices are also described). Nuer theology, as expounded by Evans-Pritchard, was different from the pre-Christian Hagen moral order in which ancestors held a pre-eminent (but not exclusive) space. For the Nuer sacrifices were directed ultimately to Kwoth, a Sky Spirit whom Evans-Pritchard wrote of as God (1956, p. 201). Ghosts of the dead (presumably kin) could also be involved, but the life of the sacrificed animal was said to be offered to God (Kwoth, 'Spirit'), even if ghosts of the dead were seen as interested parties and had to be informed, and sometimes had to be appeased if the animal was not consecrated to them by name. A rather complex theological and pragmatic dance can be discerned here in a hierarchical arrangement of spirits within the Nuer cosmos. Given the pre-existence of a superordinate category such as Kwoth in that cosmos, the transition to Christian modes of religious ritual might be expected to be relatively easy; however, as Sharon Hutchinson has shown, and as is so often the case, political issues have greatly shaped the adoption of Christianity over time in Southern Sudan, the region (and now independent state) to which the Nuer belong (Hutchinson, 1996).

Evans-Pritchard points out a feature of practice among the Nuer that was not shared by the Melpa. The Nuer were pastoralists in a fairly difficult environment, and they did not have large herds, so they often used castrated rams or he-goats instead of their precious oxen as sacrificial animals. (Oxen were also castrated before being led out for sacrifice, which suggests that the vitality of a male animal had to be diminished or removed before it could be offered to Kwoth.) Interestingly, from the point of view of how linguistic categorizations can work performatively to reorder reality, the animal sacrificed was always referred to as *yang*, a 'cow' (Evans-Pritchard, 1956, pp. 202–03). Indeed, this substitutive semantic usage was carried further in cases where no animal at all was sacrificed and instead a small type of cucumber, called *kwol yang*, 'cow's cucumber', was offered instead. The left or 'bad' half was then thrown away and the juice and seeds of the right or 'good' half would be rubbed on the sacrificer and then placed in the roofing thatch of a cattle byre or hut. This cucumber sacrifice might be presented as a temporary expedient or a kind of promise to the spirits that an actual animal would later be sacrificed.

The sacrifice ritual itself took a definite form, which Evans-Pritchard described as a 'canon' of the sacrificial 'drama' (p. 208), consisting of a sequence of four actions: first, driving a peg into the ground and tethering the animal to it, after which a libation of beer or milk or water was poured at the peg's base.

Second, the animal was rubbed with ashes as a mark of consecration. (Remarkably, this parallels in general Melpa practice with regard to pigs either sacrificed or given away in ceremonial exchanges.) In careful cultural exegesis Evans-Pritchard explains that the actions of the officiants in this stage of consecration, known as *buk*, indicate a symbolic identification with the animal itself. The officiant places his right hand on the animal's back, and the right hand for the Nuer is identified with the whole person. The ashes chosen must be ashes of cattle dung, not wood ash, and they are taken from the *gol* or homestead fire of the compound of the officiant, thus also symbolizing his person. These two features suggest strongly that the life of the animal is offered up instead of the life of the officiant; but also that in a sense the animal is imbued with a part of the officiant's personhood, which is thus also yielded up to the divinity. At the same time, this can only be a partial aspect of the phenomenon, because the animal is also eaten in festive fashion by the community. The personhood of the officiant does not enter the flesh of the animal, but goes with the life of the animal in the sacrifice and only via the ritual acts of consecration. We see here the creative power of ritual acts and their distinction from the totality of action contexts.

The next stage of the ritual of sacrifice was the invocation, call *lam*. The officiant holds up a spear and announces to Kwoth that the animal is now dedicated. He brandishes the spear as he walks up and down. Spectators comment and add to the invocation with elliptical and sometimes truncated formulae. All the statements made must be true and thus the words take on performative character which in J. L. Austin's famous terms might be recognized as illocutionary in intent (Austin, 1962).

The officiant brandished the spear in his right hand, and Evans-Pritchard explains that this was because the spear, as an extension of his right hand, also was a mark of mature masculine virility. The spear had to be a fighting spear, made of iron, and as such could be obtained only by trade from outside and was relatively scarce and valuable. Oxen for sacrifice had to be dispatched by this kind of spear; less important animals such as goats were killed simply by cutting their throats (Evans-Pritchard, 1956, pp. 202; 231–37).

One general point that Evans-Pritchard adds which resonates with Melpa practice is that all cattle are intrinsically seen as potential sacrifices to Kwoth and every killing of cattle is thus regarded as a sacrifice, even if in practice a part of the motivation has to do with the consumption of meat (Evans-Pritchard, 1956, p. 270). The same holds for pigs among the Melpa. Individual sacrifices of pigs were, and are, made on occasions of the sickness of family members, and at these events the participants need to find out by divination which ancestral spirit is upset and has caused or permitted the sickness to happen, so that the sacrifice can be properly directed. The traditional form of divination was called *el mong poromen*, 'they push in the arrow head', and only the ritual specialist known as a *mön wuö*, 'spell man', could perform it. This specialist vigorously pushed an arrow through the rear bark wall of a men's house and asked the spirits of dead kin to seize onto the arrowhead if they wished to affirm responsibility for the sickness of the patient. What kind of pig was to be sacrificed was then determined, again by the putative response of the spirit implicated. The kinsfolk would next have to find the right kind of pig (by colour, sex) as indicated. With Christian conversion from the 1930s onwards, pork sacrifices came into question. The idea was that God did not require sacrifices (making him unlike the Nuer Kwoth), but prayers should be made to him for blessings or healing. However, the imperative to kill pigs in sacrifice is so strong that meetings to discuss reasons for a sickness and to make prayers for the patient's recovery would scarcely be considered effective without such a mediating intervention as only such a sacrifice can bring about. This is particularly because the influence of dead kin is still felt to be powerful and close to hand in people's lives, and it may even be thought that God works through ancestors and the ancestors have not changed their predilection for pork, in spite of the teachings of churches that good Christians go to Heaven. It is enough for pigs to be killed without necessarily calling out to the dead, since as with the Nuer every such killing is implicitly a sacrifice.

Ethnographic expositions of the preceding kind for the Nuer and the Melpa are useful for helping us to understand the versatility and flexibility of sacrifice as ritual practice. We have reviewed general theories of sacrifice elsewhere (e.g. Strathern and Stewart, 2008a and b, q.v.). An alternative set of theories, grounded in evolutionary theory, can be found in the work of Christopher Palmer and his co-authors (e.g. Palmer et al., 2006).

The core idea of sacrifice, shared among otherwise quite diverse theories, is that it involves yielding up something valuable in a ritualized context, in order to ameliorate some adverse condition. We have dealt here with animal sacrifice, which involves the killing of living creatures as substitutes for humans. A transformation of this practice is when persons who die in combat fighting for their group are said to have offered themselves as a sacrifice. The return is not for them, but for their group; or, since they are given honour, their social persona and the memory of it are enhanced and perhaps added to family prestige. Such an unmediated or direct sacrifice may reproduce the category of the hero. Dying for the faith, in religious contexts, produces a homologous kind of hero, as a martyr. A variant of such violent forms of sacrifice was explored by René Girard in his book *Violence and the Sacred* (1977). Girard took his cue from the substitutive function of the animal sacrificed. If the animal stands for a human person and is substituted for them (as in the Old Testament 'a ram caught in a thicket'), then the original victim would be a human of the community itself. Girard suggested that this background might help to explain why animal sacrifice is sometimes linked to a certain aura of guilt (not that this is in fact universal). Hence the animal takes away the possibility of violence ('murder') within that community, and it becomes in effect a scapegoat, carrying away putative evil and defusing violent actions between humans. Sacrifice requires a surrogate victim (Girard, 1977, p. 101), and the whole community is purified through it. Girard's theorizing is shot through with its background in classical Greek and Judaeo-Christian traditions and themes, and the idea of violence is central to it. It undoubtedly has application to such traditions and resonances with other traditions, such as those of the Nuer and the Dinka studied by Evans-Pritchard (above) and Lienhardt (Girard, pp. 97–99; Lienhardt, 1961). For Girard, however, as is shown in his title, a central concept is violence, whereas for Evans-Pritchard and Lienhardt the central concept is sacrificial substitution itself, or in the case of the Dinka the self-immolation of some Dinka ritual experts (masters of the fishing-spear) on behalf of the whole community.

The noted classical scholar Walter Burkert held that sacrificial practices arose from the killing of animals in the hunt by hunter-and-gatherer populations in prehistoric times. He also saw continuities running from such times into ancient Greek practices as described by Homer and in the origins of Greek tragedy. He argued, inter alia, that the traditions of a goat-sacrifice associated with this dramatic art form were reflected in the very word itself, *tragoidia* (meaning perhaps goat-song and referring to dancers dressed as goats, or songs sung at the sacrifice of a goat) (Burkert, 2001). Burkert's work clearly illustrates the focus on animal sacrifice that runs through scholarly investigations, possibly because of the compelling general human interest in the confrontation of life with death (see Burkert, p. 21, the last words in this chapter of his book *Savage Energies*).

Kathryn McClymond, by contrast, has reviewed the broader field of practices relating to sacrificial offerings in an explicit effort to get away from the fascination with blood-sacrifice and animal death (McClymond, 2008). Her methodological approach is twofold. First, she takes a polythetic pathway into the definition of what sacrifice is, seeing it as a field of possibilities in which some actions appear more obviously sacrificial in character than others. Second, she points out that sacrificial offerings may include vegetable and liquid substances, as well as animal. She also makes the point (that has often independently occurred to us in our role as ethnographers of New Guinea cultures) that a killing is not necessarily seen by its participants as a violent killing, that is, one whose legitimacy is contested if we follow the definitions offered by David Riches (Riches, 1986). Citing the much discussed Yom Kippur rite of slaughtering one male goat while sending another into the wilderness 'for Azazel', McClymond argues that both the slaughter and the sending away are equally acts of sacrificial purification, so that killing is only one part of a complex two-step ritual procedure (McClymond, pp. 63–64; see also the discussions in Douglas, 1999 and Janowitz, 2011). In further contexts grain may be offered in lieu of living creatures or vegetal offerings may themselves be primary gifts. Grain may be processed into flour and cakes or porridge in types of sacrificial cooking (McClymond, p. 71). In Vedic rituals grain cakes could be shared out into parts for the deities and for the human celebrants (ibid.). The Vedic deity Prajapati is said to have created this type of cake as a part of rituals to overcome death (p. 71). Plants and animals were all seen as sharing the same juice or life force (p. 72). It is important to note, then, that plants too may be seen as 'killed' in sacrifices (McClymond, p. 129). The juice of the plant is like the blood of an animal. In some ways, this detracts from the narrower significance of McClymond's argument, but in a much broader and more important way it confirms the validity of her position because it highlights the fact that it is the cosmic context as imagined by the people themselves that holds the clues to the proper understanding of what we call sacrifice.

Sacrifice is one of the grand themes in anthropological theorizing. In the next chapter we examine some of the more recent foci of particular investigations of ritual acts, regardless of their particular substantive loci as sacrifice, initiation, social drama, conflict settlement, divination or other categories of activity.

6

Contemporary approaches
to ritual analysis

The phenomenon of ritual in social life attracts a wide variety of approaches to it as an object of study, for example: Cochrane, 2013; Kreinath, 2012b; Pedersen, 2006; Scott, 2007 and Stewart and Strathern, 2005, 2007. In this book we have already explored a number of such approaches, starting with the ideas of classicists, including Sir James Frazer, and moving on through twentieth-century structural-functional hypotheses to the creative extrapolations from these made by Victor and Edith Turner, beginning with the concept of social drama and then introducing the notions of liminality and communitas. We moved next to the classic themes of sacrifice and divination, drawing on the foundational work of Meyer Fortes and Edward Evans-Pritchard on the Tallensi and the Nuer peoples, and capping this with some reflections on Katherine McClymond's salutary reminder that not all sacrifices are blood sacrifices nor need they be considered primarily as acts of violence. In some cultural contexts animals that are hunted are thought of as offering themselves as sacrifices to those who hunt them, so that the act of killing them can be seen as a respectful act of acceptance of an offering willingly made. The example shows how important interpretations are. An act that from an external viewpoint might be seen as violent or aggressive may be interpreted differently when seen from the viewpoint of the participants themselves.

Secrecy in ritual practices

Anthropology entered the sphere of interpretive work as a part of an evolution away from structural-functional analyses (which were also interpretive in their way) and into a varied suite of attempts to understand rituals from the perspectives of a number of themes. The first theme we will take up here is the theme of ritual secrecy. Many ritual practices involve a restricted number of participants, a demonstration of symbols of power or meaning to participants and a corresponding transformation in the status of the participants as they emerge from the ritual itself. Van Gennep's rites of passage model clearly comes into mind here, as does Victor Turner's social drama insofar as it involves a period of seclusion of the participants in the drama.

We want to look here at the different meanings that may cluster around the issue of secrecy in rituals. The basic concept at work is that rituals are implicated in the construction of power between people, and the acquisition or exercise of power is thought of as occurring in and through secret acts that mark their participants off from others. This theme is not, of course, unique to ritual practices, since it applies to all cases when a small in-group exercises power through means that are not shared outside of the in-group itself.

Another point, however, also applies. This is that secrecy belongs only to a certain phase of the ritual (or political, or economic) phase. The power itself often has to be exhibited in public contexts of its revelation even if its underpinnings remain hidden. This is why, of course, initiates must come out of their seclusion, in order to demonstrate their acquisition of power in the shape of physical maturity, attractiveness, knowledge, status or the like. Secrecy goes hand in hand with the importance of revelation, although what is revealed may be the product of power rather than the source of power itself, which may remain hidden, and kept in the control of the group that claims it (e.g. in sacred stones that are buried secretly in the ground of a ritual site).

Power also can refer to different things. Cosmic or religious power may be exercised on behalf of the whole group, or it may be turned to secret, illegitimate or contested ends, such as in forms of sorcery, including assault sorcery (see Strathern and Stewart, 2011, pp. 24–48). Secrecy in these circumstances acquires a different meaning in political interactional terms, since it is used as a method of attack on others rather than as an internal preliminary to a positive revelation of well-being at a community level.

In this chapter we are going to draw on two separate studies of the significance of secrecy in ritual practices. The first comes from fieldwork conducted in neighbouring social contexts in the West Sepik or Sandaun Province in Papua New Guinea by Bernard Juillerat and Alfred Gell. At issue between the two ethnographers was the question of the exegetical meanings assigned to the ritual practices that were identical or similar in both communities, the Yangis ritual cycle among the Yafar whom Juillerat studied over many years, and the Umeda studied by Gell. Relying on detailed exegeses given to him by two ritual specialists in ·arcane knowledge, whose names he also had to keep secret, Juillerat was able to place much of the symbolism of the Yangis into a broad overall cosmic scheme of practices centring on growth, fertility, decay and maternal relations (e.g. Juillerat, 1992). In addition, Juillerat added a further interpretive twist of his own, bringing into alignment Yafar practices and a Freudian interpretation depending on the concept of the Oedipus complex (on this see Strathern and Stewart, 2010a). We are not concerned with this Freudian approach further here, other than to say that it reveals the many layers of interpretive thinking that may feed into an anthropological text, ranging from the communications by the participants to the remote analytical purviews brought to bear from some outside perspective. Also, in the case of Freudian theorizing, the ethnographic data might be expected to be opaque to interpretation because the true meanings are expected to be repressed in the unconscious of the actors and so by definition would not enter into their exegesis.

What we are concerned with, however, is the meaning or function of secrecy itself. The Yangis/Ida complex of rituals is not in itself wholly secret. On the contrary, the decorations and dance displays occur in a plaza and are watched by enthusiastic spectators. The participants dress elaborately, with much use of body paint, feathers and natural items from the environment. The whole point is to provide an image of festivity, well-being and renewal. In a very general sense, Gell and Juillerat, predictably enough, agreed on this starting point for analysis. Where they diverged was in terms of how they further pursued their interpretations of their data. As he explains in his contribution to Juillerat's edited collection of studies on Ritual and Meaning centring on Yangis/Ida, Gell states that he does not think 'that there is an overall mythical exegesis of the pattern of the Ida ritual as a whole' (1992, p. 128). Instead, he adheres to the idea of an observer's model guided by his sociological imagination (ibid.). At the same time, he admits that 'secret exegetical lore' may well feed into an observer's model of the kind he developed. For the Ida, in turn, he raises the question of the centrality of the dancing figures known as *eli*, or cassowaries, and asks why the Yafar ritual experts had no secret exegesis for these striking characters. In Gell's view the important thing was that the *eli* were cassowaries, senior male figures who were to be replaced by the younger generation of the *ipele* bowmen. Juillerat, however, saw them as ritual figures who represented the generation of the mothers that would give way over time to the generation of their daughters (Juillerat, 1992, pp. 27–28). In both interpretations generational symbolism is postulated, but Juillerat notes that Yafar informants did not identify the *eri* (= *eli*) as cassowaries (p. 28). Juillerat also did not claim that there was a complete logical system of symbols at work, but he made maximum productive use of the exegesis provided to him by special experts who controlled access to the knowledge of the work of creating a 'sexualized cosmos' carried out by two deities (p. 25). In this cosmic order two concepts were fundamental: *hoofuk*, meaning inner core, pith, vital force, reproductive power, and *roofuk*, meaning the skin, or tree bark, or an envelope or covering (p. 26). Yangis dancers were said to show *hoofuk* power, which 'bears a dominantly female connotation' (p. 27). A good part of this exegesis was given to Juillerat because of his married status – he had entered the world of reproduction – whereas it was denied to Gell because at the time he was a young bachelor and not entitled to know these secrets. Secrecy, therefore, as with the Baktaman studied by Fredrik Barth (Barth, 1975, 1987), was highly stratified, and control of knowledge was synonymous with the task of maintaining the cosmos. Since the Yafar had borrowed the Ida rituals (renaming them Yangis) from the Punda, neighbours of the Umeda, it seems inevitable that this ritual knowledge was passed on secretly from Umeda/Punda experts to qualified elders in Yafar.

If the background knowledge about the origins of Ida/Yangis was the same or substantially the same, we may ask why this knowledge had to be secret rather than equally shared. The answer to this question takes a form which goes beyond the two cases in point. It is very common in New Guinea cultures for the idea of the cosmos to be based upon an occult source of power which has periodically to be revealed or made visible and operational for society to be renewed and strengthened. Both the occult or latent aspect and the public or active aspect of power are important, they go together as a sort of elementary structure (an atom of ritual like Lévi-Strauss's atom of kinship), or an elementary structure, again, in Lévi-Strauss's terms (Lévi-Strauss, 1963, p. 72, 1969).

The studies by Gell and Juillerat generated a large corpus of further interpretations and comments (see Juillerat, 1992 again, and A. Strathern, 1992 in that volume). Among these commentators, many of whom seemed to think they could understand the rituals better than either of the two ethnographers by wielding their own favourite analytical tools, the most thoughtful in methodological terms was perhaps Donald Tuzin, when he addressed the issue of exegesis. Juillerat accorded exegesis a special value as a way of bridging over from public and deeper meanings. Tuzin asks what of those cases where people cannot, or will not, provide an exegesis? (Tuzin, 1992, p. 253). Surely, he suggests, there must be ways of getting at 'meanings' of ritual acts even in the absence of explanations by informants? Or what if the exegeses offered by specialists have little bearing on the view of the ordinary participants in the ritual? Tuzin answers the second of these questions by noting that what is significant here is that some people keep meaning secret or esoteric but do so on behalf of the larger group. Secrecy means some people are excluded. It is a marker of group identity. As for the generation of meanings Tuzin follows Barth (1987): meanings are generated as a process out of experience (p. 259), they are not complete, but are a project, unfinished, but also patently creative. Tuzin's first question can often be reframed by noting that there is more than one way of getting at exegeses without 'training' the informants to reply in terms meaningful only to the questioner. We can observe ritual actions and build up a picture of how they are patterned. And often by hitting on a way of talking, the anthropologist can simply elicit something that had been previously withheld.

In circumstances of induced change, it is clear that another context of secrecy emerges. Actions that have been proscribed by government or missions may 'go underground'. People hide them. They become secret, or more secret than they were. Practitioners may deny their existence while tenaciously holding to them, either in an original or a transformed way.

Summing up the discussion so far, we can say that secrecy is a way of producing and storing power, but this power can only be made operational when its products are revealed in visible and tangible form, in dances and sacrifices, for example. Ritual actions then become vehicles of resistance to change. They may also be vehicles of change themselves, as they camouflage and adapt themselves, and they may come to encompass 'modern' forms of symbolism, as in the New Guinea cargo cults (e.g. Lawrence, 1964). Christian Højbjerg has given us a detailed and sensitive picture of 'the local strategic use of concealed religious knowledge' among the Loma of South-East Guinea (Højbjerg, 2007, p. 40). As we ourselves have noted above, and in line with previous writings (e.g. Simmel, 1991), Højbjerg notes that secrecy is meaningful only when it can be at least partially revealed. The category of secrets he is concerned with are called *sale*. Knowledge of *sale* is acquired through apprenticeship, and practitioners join together in hierarchically organized cult societies in which some members are acknowledged to have superior *sale* knowledge. Interestingly, Højbjerg points out that 'much secret knowledge is actually known by those who are excluded from sharing this knowledge' (p. 41). True secrets, by contrast, tend to consist of recipes for *sale* herbal medicines or magic (ibid.). In contrast to matters of verbal exegesis, secrecy consists largely in 'physical contact with the ritual objects' that outsiders must not see or touch (pp. 41–42). This is an important observation that undoubtedly has application to New Guinea practices, for example, practices surrounding sacred stones in the Female Spirit rituals in Mount Hagen, Papua New Guinea (Strathern and Stewart, 1999a; Stewart and Strathern, 2002a, pp. 165–209). Seeing the Spirit in the form of decorated stones is an important part of the rituals, and seeing these stones entails in turn cooking pork sacrifices in the ritual enclosure set off from the sight of all but the male celebrants and the ritual master guiding them, and rubbing the stones with pork fat to increase fertility. Cult initiates are *koepa köni*, 'those who have cooked and seen', while others are *koepa nö köni*, 'those who have not cooked or seen'.

A dramatic aspect of secrecy and revelation among the Loma is provided by elaborate masking rituals, in which masked figures emerge from secret places and reveal themselves in the open. These masks are in effect whole body costumes. They cover the person, who assumes the identity of the mask for the duration of the performance. Masks incorporate external histories and internal complementarities and oppositions between males and females, since they are always made by males but are related to ideas of women's power also. They hide one identity and reveal another, that of the mask itself. They are appropriate vehicles for producing a transformation of social role of the performer, whose identity at the end of a performance is now different from the time when he prepared in secrecy to wear the mask-costume. The mask both conceals and reveals the performers (Højbjerg, pp. 204 ff.).

Sale practices have been proscribed by state authorities, who presumably see them as politically subversive. Secret religious objects have been brought out into the open by these authorities in an attempt to deny and destroy their secret power. Højbjerg notes, however, the subtlety of responses to this 'state iconoclasm'. The secret *knowledge* about the objects is not revealed, so their power is not actually destroyed. We may also suggest here that when spirits are involved and the objects are dwellings for the spirits, if the spirits are not brought outside but stay inside then the religious source of power remains intact. Ritual logics have to be understood, therefore, in their own precise terms.

Rituals as ritual

Approaches to the understanding of ritual have tended to fluctuate over time. Emile Durkheim (Durkheim, 1965) saw religion, and therefore its rituals, as the energized modality of society itself; Radcliffe-Brown, in an essentially similar mode, looked for the functions of rituals in maintaining social structure and values (Radcliffe-Brown, 1952); Lévi-Strauss sought to discern in myths (if not rituals) fundamental classifications of the world (Lévi-Strauss, 1978); processualists and their successors tried increasingly to elucidate the meanings brought to play in ritual processes (e.g. as in the work of Turner, 1969). Progressively, we can see here a cumulative turn towards meanings as internally expressed in rituals themselves. The logical conclusion of this turn to lived and experienced meanings is to be found in the volume edited by Don Handelman and Galena Lindquist, on *Ritual in Its Own Right* (2004).

In their Preface to that volume the editors briefly refer to their overall inspiration for the book: suspicion of the view of ritual as a form of representation, and a wish to deal with 'the interior organization of ritual', also, a search for the dynamics of ritual (2004, viii). Handelman elaborates further in the Introduction on these somewhat vatic pronouncements. He suggests that a ritual practice should first be separated analytically from its sociocultural surrounding context, and then should be reinserted back into its context, with the knowledge gained by taking the first step (Handelman, 2004, p. 4). The aim here seems to be to determine how far the ritual can be seen as autonomous, and how far it must be related to 'sociocultural order' in order for it to be understood (ibid.). Another matter in which Handelman is interested is the extent to which ritual is 'self-organizing' (ibid.) – a phrase that goes with the idea of autonomy, and perhaps with the adjective 'autocatalytic' (self-producing or self-generating).

Later Handelman also writes of 'self-integrity, the interior capacity of phenomena to sustain themselves' (p. 10). He adverts further to phenomena as self-referential or self-reflexive (p. 11). Finally, he relates all this to the 'subjunctive character' of autopoiesis, seemingly echoing Victor Turner's idea of rituals as creating 'as if' conditions or possible worlds in themselves.

Handelman is fond of using vivid images to produce a metaphorical picture of the meanings he wants to give to ritual. What he is writing about here can perhaps be explicated by a brief discussion of the Female Spirit rituals in the Highlands of Papua New Guinea. These were rituals historically directed toward gaining fertility and prosperity from a powerful Female Spirit belonging to a class of mythological

Sky Beings seen as the first givers of power to human kinship groups. We have detailed the rituals performed inside a cult enclosure many times in previous publications (e.g. Strathern and Stewart, 1999a; Stewart and Strathern, 2002a). It is sufficient here to say that the basic dynamic of the ritual is that the immediate celebrants were males of the group holding the performance, who entered and exited the enclosure in sets of pairs, one partner being called the 'women's house side' and the other the 'men's house side', thus constituting an elementary structure of alliance within a framework of descent – collapsing descent and alliance into each other, in effect. Inside the enclosure the spatializing of ritual co-operative action followed the same logic of division plus alliance. The overall performance consisted of taking ritual paraphernalia into the enclosure at various times from outside, transforming these paraphernalia by sacrificial cooking, and emerging as brightly decorated dancers celebrating the Spirit by wearing her emblems, including the White Bird of Paradise plumes (*köi kuri*) and distributing copious quantities of cooked pork to massive crowds of spectators. Women did not enter the enclosure because the Spirit was said to be jealous of them: within the enclosure all the men were said to be married polyandrously to the Spirit, reversing the order of polygyny that held outside the enclosure. The materials the men carried in, however, were a mixture of the results of male and female labour – field crops, forest leaves and ferns, pork for sacrifices. Once taken in, they were ritually transformed by cooking, and partly taken out again for distribution to the large crowds of visitors. This simple ethnographic description shows that there was a dynamic of movement from outside to inside and vice versa. The structure of relationality was peculiar to the cult, yet it also replicated aspects of outside organization in a condensed form. The 'meaning' of this dynamic lies, therefore, precisely in the imposition of outside on inside and inside on outside: what Handelman called 'self-closure' on one hand and 'twisting back' on the other (Handelman, 2004, p. 17). Handelman would regard this cult as a relatively simple case, since it clearly does replicate (if not 'reflect') outside structures of pairing and alliance; but note the reversals: the paired males, called men's house and women's house sides, contain both genders in themselves, whereas the rules of entry into the enclosure separate males and females. The Spirit is Female and takes many husbands;

outside of the enclosure men practice polygyny. So what do all of these reversals lead to? Surely they construct the categories of alliance by pairing which actually are important in the social structure at large. By creating its own world, the cult also recreates the wider world outside. And the boundary of inside/outside is actually very important. The fence has a special name, *kor röprö*, the Spirit's barrier. Pace Handelman (p. 27) boundaries can be important even if there is an obvious relationship between the inside and the outside. The one does not *represent* the other, though. Rather, the aim of the overall ritual is clear and singular: to increase fertility by enacting a pageant of complementaity built out of apparent opposites. This formulation in turn escapes Handelman's dichotomous view of 'ritual' versus 'society'. Our whole discussion here re-instantiates a previous argument we have made about the 'collaborative model' of gender relations that we put forward on the basis of the Female Spirit materials (e.g. Stewart and Strathern, 1999).

Bruce Kapferer takes up the cudgel against 'representation' as a feature of ritual which he receives from Handelman (Kapferer, 2004). Instead of representation as a core theme, Kapferer offers us 'virtuality', which he says is actually 'a thorough going reality of its own' (p. 37), and is a concentration of dynamic forces in which 'the distinct capacities of human consciousness and mind and the potentialities of human creativity . . . are revealed' (p. 39). Kapferer's concept of 'ritual dynamics' works well enough as an expression of the force that participants feel is generated through ritual. If we take the Female Spirit rituals again, the culminating dance in which the participants stream out of the enclosure and perform the swift foot-drumming dance that shakes the earth and is hailed by those waiting outside as 'The Spirit is Coming!' (*kor onom*), is precisely an example of this kind of force, exerted at the climax of the embodied visual performance. Since the dance is distinctively different from *any* other context, ritual or everyday, it also corresponds to what Kapferer refers to 'as a radical suspension of ordinary realities' (p. 46); but we would contend that the rite does in fact merge into the functioning polity at large because it creates and sustains social alliances that last beyond the time of performance itself. The ritual is not a film or a play, but it is an 'integrator', we may say.

Let us take Kapferer's formulation of ritual as a form of 'virtuality' here (Kapferer, p. 46). He writes that ritual has 'no essential representational symbolic relation to external realities'; also that it is a 'self-contained imaginal space' (p. 47). For him, this type of virtuality must be seen as 'really real' (p. 47), and non-referential to external reality. It is a deep kind of reality, revealing important dimensions of experience, one could say, as did Greek tragic drama. (Kapferer rejects the comparison with theatre and does not like the idea that ritual is the primordial form of theatre, but reflection on what Greek tragic drama was like might lead us to rethink this point, see Chapter 2 in this book.)

From time to time in his analysis Kapferer, like Handelman, agrees that ritual dynamics can flow over into life beyond the ritual itself. However, he is committed to seeing ritual and life outside of ritual as existentially dichotomous. He also dislikes the term process for its supposed flat, linear character. But if we return to our Female Spirit example, we get another angle on this whole discussion. At the end of the performance, the male participants bring out their sacred cooked pork and *distribute* it to *everyone*, specifically jamming pieces onto a forest of upturned spears as they stand on a high platform, the *kor ropoklama*, 'spirit platform'. The dynamic force of the pork goes out into the whole gathering of people. They take it away. Inside and outside are conjoined. This *is a ritual process*. It has a telos, an ending, that affirms the transcendent unity of inside and outside. It is a holistic message that negates a dichotomy. It is also the culmination of the 'really real' in the collective embodiment of diffuse power. There is in effect nothing virtual here at all. It is all simply real. The idea of the 'virtual' suggests that there is some disjunction between the cult performance inside the enclosure and the outside world, but this is not actually what is happening. The ritual *is* a process, and a dynamic one at that, and it takes both linear and circular forms, integrating various domains of relationship. We do not need an idea of the virtual here. It seems, indeed, a vestige of the real versus unreal distinction even while Kapferer denies this to be the case. If ritual is to be seen 'in its own right' – an aim that is certainly admirable – there is no need to divide it off from the rest of reality, because truly, in spite of its phenomenological separation from the everyday, it is deeply integrated with it; and for the Female Spirit ritual, pork is the prime integrator and marker of this effectivity.

Ritual failures

This topic will bridge over into the theme of the next chapter, on performance and performativity. 'Failure' is a concept that can have various meanings. Even failures at exams may be complex in character and a product of subjective thoughts and biases. In the case of rituals, we have to ask from whose viewpoint is the failure supposed to have occurred and what was its character? If the purposes of a ritual are highly specific and clearly targeted, a measurement of success may be possible, but over what time span? If the purposes are very general, assessment may be much harder. Multiple functions may be invoked, as in the proverbial tag 'Well, it didn't bring rain, but it was one hell of a ceremony!'

Nevertheless, circumstances do occur when the participants say a ritual went wrong and / or failed to produce its intended effects. In the Female Spirit rituals an expert may be criticized for setting up the sacred site or a part of it incorrectly, resulting in sickness in the celebrating group rather than prosperity and health. A ritual supposed to create peace may end in renewed conflict, fisticuffs, and accusations of further wrongdoings, notably when a promised compensation payment is deemed insufficient.

In his Introduction to the volume *When Rituals Go Wrong* (Hüsken ed., 2007), E. L. Schieffelin reported on an earlier article of his (Schieffelin, 1996, mentioned in Schieffelin, 2007) in which he examined the failure of performance by a spirit medium in a séance among the Kaluli people of Papua New Guinea. While the séance as a whole was not said to have failed, this particular spirit medium's performance was said to have collapsed. The medium's failure therefore did not cause the whole ritual to be said to have failed. Here, then we have a failure of commission, but only by one performer. In other cases, the failure of correct performance by a single practitioner may threaten the whole ritual sequence, as when a Female Spirit specialist sets up a site wrongly and the Spirit is seemingly annoyed and sends sickness rather than health to the community. On the other hand purely devotional rituals with no specified expectation of outcome may require strict rules of performance but without fears of a loss of efficacy in cases where the rules are not completely followed. Even so, in such cases, because of the rigid specification of the rules themselves and the idea that breaking them annoys the deities to whom they are directed, specialists may be equipped to make ritual repairs by way of atonements and remedies. This what a succeeding specialist would do in cases of wrong installations for the Female Spirit ritual or the Male Spirit ritual in Hagen. In the latter, a specialist was supposed to identify a spring and channel it into a prescribed flow through the site. The spring was supposed to have two 'eyes', one called 'open', the other 'closed', and the spring water had to follow the channel made for it. If it broke out from the channel, the ritual was spoiled. The remedy was therefore to repair the channel and make a new sacrifice in the site (Stewart and Strathern, 2001, pp. 90–112).

Another source of trouble that Schieffelin cites is from the chapter by Buss in the volume. Newly dead persons' spirits seek to find their way to the land of the dead but may be hindered by disturbed ghosts who ambush them and take their food from them. Buss's study is on the Newar people of Nepal, and the idea of the hungry ghost is of course famously shared by Chinese ritualists in their lineage-based sacrifices. Proper feeding of both the living and the dead is the foundation of cosmic order in such rituals, and hungry ghosts are a marker of cosmic disorder, as Buss points out (Buss, 2007). We ourselves have been privileged in 2010 to take part in rituals for the reconsecration of a village lineage temple on the island of Jinmen belonging to Taiwan. Some of the rituals also coincided with winter solstice celebrations in which foods are set out on family household altars on the top floors of dwellings. Family members, including our student helper and co-investigator Ms Kuang-ting Chuang, advised that the offerings must be set out and notionally consumed by the family kin before noon, otherwise hungry and disgruntled ghosts from outside might arrive and steal the life substance of the offerings, thus imperiling the household welfare. The family, therefore, are responsible for seeing that the offerings are made ready, and prayers, burnings of incense and paper money are all made in good time and in correct ways. Their well-being is at stake.

In general, the issue of 'failure' (versus 'mishap' or 'unexpected adversity'), must depend on close ethnographic reading of the data, and should not be uncritically imported into an account as an observer's construct without checking what the participants' views are, Schieffelin notes (p. 11). Schieffelin further notes that a deviation from standard practice may act as an innovation and the readoption and later abandonment of a ritual practice may implicate wider political changes in people's sensibilities. He cites Michael Rudolph's chapter on the Atayal indigenous group in Taiwan who restored a previous ritual with the approval of the local Christian church authorities but abandoned it later under the pressure of the same church. The issues surrounding this process led to a wider development of political consciousness among the Atayal people vis-à-vis the Han dominated state (pp. 11–12). This example illustrates a wider set of points made by Schieffelin in his thoughtful Introduction to the *When Rituals Go Wrong* volume, that what constitutes failure rather than success may be ambiguous or uncertain, and that indirect outcomes may lead into success in other domains of historical action. Schieffelin also stresses that such questions are set into political competition between rivals, as in several of the studies in that volume, for example, the study by Ute Hüsken of a contemporary Indian temple dedicated to Vishnu and Christiane Brosius's chapter on a pilgrimage organized by the VHP Hindu political party to take a stone pillar to a contested ritual site of a famous old mosque. (Studies of this sort contrast strongly with any contexts in which a model of ritual antagonism balanced by some kind of tolerance of the other side's presence on the site can be plausibly applied.)

'Mistakes' form another category, along with 'failure', that can have an effect on ritual practices. Stephen Frankel, in his study of the Huli people of Papua New Guinea, referred to the story that a ritual mistake had occurred in an earth-renewing (*dindi gamu*) ritual among these people, when a light-skinned boy called Bayebaye from the neighbouring Duna people was accidentally killed. Since the earth-renewing rituals among both Duna and Huli involved sacrifices to chthonian ancestral figures, the image of this killing, accidental or not, carries clear resonances with themes of sacrificial killings in general. This story of Bayebaye later on became mixed up with Christian themes of the crucifixion of Jesus, since Bayebaye was said to have been 'light-skinned' (see Stewart and Strathern, 2002b, pp. 70–72). Here, a narrative of a 'mistake' blends into a wider sacrificial theme and later into an introduced Christian cosmology (for further details see Frankel, 1986, p. 23; Glasse, 1995, pp. 57–86). The example underscores the complexities underlining stories about the effects of rituals, to which we turn in the next chapter.

7

Performance and performativity

The terms performance and performativity are derived, at least in part, from theorizing in the field of linguistic anthropology. In linguistic theory performance is distinguished from competence. Competence refers to the capacity to speak or write in accordance with rules of the language, while performance refers to the actual patterns of use of the language, which may deviate from or exceed minimal competence. The scholar Dell Hymes introduced the further notion of communicative competence, the knowledge required for a speaker to function effectively as a member of a social group or speech community. The emphasis here was not simply on knowledge but the ability to communicate with others in acceptable ways. Because performances can vary in terms of their effectiveness and appeal, this means that an aesthetic element is present, and this element comes into being through the valuations placed on speech (or literacy) events. Hence, performance implies also creativity and the ability to improvise to fit an occasion, whether it may be conversation, speech-making, or the production of songs and music. At this point performance clearly intersects with rituals (see Duranti, 1997, pp. 14–15 for an exposition along the above lines). We have already noted, in discussing the work on ritual by Victor Turner, how his concept of the social drama and its ritualized forms clearly implied that rituals were performances intended for spectators and participants as a heightened presentation of experience. Turner's work on pilgrimages followed this line of thought, and further bound together the category of performance with the anthropology of experience. As an example, dramas by definition involve a heightening of experience and senses of participation and rituals classically either accomplish such a heightening or aim to do so.

When we consider performance in the light of its attendant effects, we are bridging over into the arena of performativity. Ronald Grimes, following the famous work by the philosopher J. L. Austin (Austin, 1962), developed the field of ritual criticism by taking Austin's categories of speech acts and applying these to ritual acts (which, of course, may also either involve speech or be speech acts, as in Austin's own examples). Grimes developed a typology of 'infelicitous performances', borrowing this term from Austin's own writings (Grimes, 1996, p. 283). Austin, he says, distinguished between constative and performative speech acts (*autrement dit* 'locutionary' and 'illocutionary' or 'perlocutionary' speech acts and their effects). Austin recognized the following kinds of infelicities or breaches: misfires, abuses, non-plays, misapplications, flaws, omissions, misframes, and a number of other detailed categories (Grimes, pp. 285–88). Grimes also lists hitches, insincerities, violations, breaches, glosses and flops (p. 286). And he notes a general category of 'ineffectualities' which he defines as 'procedures that fail to bring about intended changes' (ibid.). This last formulation broaches most crucially the question of performativity, because it recognizes that a ritual (like any other social act or event, we should add) may 'fail', as in the examples from Ute Hüsken's edited volume cited in the previous chapter of this book. The category of failing is, however, rather broad, and rituals may fail in one regard and succeed, at least partially, in another. Indeed, there may be no way of absolutely measuring their success other than via subjective feelings of satisfaction or otherwise on the side of participants. Grimes cites an ethnographic example of a shaman among the Mazatec people who was unable to heal a patient and acknowledged sadness at the end of a chant. Yet surely, all doctors recognize this possibility. Grimes notes that the chant may in any case have prepared the kinsfolk for the loss of life and their grief at this. Also, a model based entirely on intentions tends to ignore the results that are similar to Austin's perlocutionary effects, that is, unintended but beneficial effects. By implication a focus on intentions also excludes observers' reckonings of the possible functions of a ritual event, and hence all functionalist debates about these.

There has been some discussion about the meaning of the term performativity. As we use it here, it can cover both intended and unintended results of actions that are seen as performances. A useful addition to this thematic arena is made by Susanna Rostas, who distinguishes between ritualization and performativity (Rostas, 1998, pp. 85–104). Both are seen as parts of ritual process. Ritualization is the process of embodiment that produces ritual action (= Catherine Bell's and Pierre Bourdieu's ideas of the ritualized body). It is not necessarily conscious. Performativity, for Rostas, however, is consciously intensified performance, which produces strong aesthetic effects. While this is not exactly the meaning we give to the term performativity, Rostas's suggestions feed well into general performativity theory. Performativity has to do with *effects*. How are these effects produced or not produced? Certainly performativity relates to the idea of the 'felicitous performance' we have just discussed. If we take the example of dances celebrating ritual exchanges of wealth in Mount Hagen, Papua New Guinea, we can see how this works. The dancers on the side of those holding the exchange and giving wealth away are supposed to be elaborately and aesthetically decorated. They are supposed to execute the dance movements well and to sing strongly in harmony. If the spectators do not see the dancers as having achieved theses aims, they will say that the group has fallen out of favour with the ancestors and one of their number may die, because of some internal wrongdoing. The wealth goods (pigs, shells, money) may be given away successfully, but the overall performativity of the event is reduced (see above, Chapter 6, on the question of partial failures). Performativity may belong to different domains of action. In the example just given, overall political prestige (comparable to symbolic capital in the terms of Bourdieu, 1977) may hinge on the quality of decorations worn by the dancers, while economic capital or financial stability is expressed (achieved) in the numbers and condition of pigs given away to partners. Ultimately, for the Hageners these two facets of success are codependent, since the luster of decorations depends on the ability to persuade helpers to loan the finery required, and this can happen only if there is socio-cosmic trust underpinning all ritual and practical activities. (In this sense there is no dichotomy between ritual and practical spheres, they form a conjoined whole.)

We have previously examined the question of performativity in two articles published in the *Journal of Ritual Studies* and in the *Reader on Ritual* (Strathern and Stewart, 2008c, 2008d; Stewart and Strathern, 2010). In the first of these pieces we took cases from three different areas well known for their traditions of shamanic practices. Each of these cases brought out aspects of practice important for assessing performativity. The first case was from the Yukaghir of Siberia, among whom shamans were involved in enhancing the activities of hunters by imitating the movements of animals hunted and drawing them to the hunter, thus enabling them to be killed. In the animistic cosmos of the Yukaghir, the performativity of the shaman's powers of embodied mimesis enabled hunting to be successful. This example stresses the importance of understanding the local cosmic culture and its influence on embodied action in determining performativity.

The second case was from Korea, where shamans have been historically very important as healers, even though their profession has sometimes been denigrated or even stigmatized. According to the study we used, by Kim, shamans survive by operating in experiential fields outside of biomedicine, explaining illness in terms of misfortune and bad luck (rather than, e.g. disease). In their practice, shamans provide a 'framework for transformation' of experience that gives a basis for healing, for example, explaining the causes of illness by the use of divination sticks to discover which spirits have been displeased and sent the illness. This classic pattern is another way in which performativity is achieved, because the shaman's ritual action meets a need which other modalities of action do not, and cannot, provide. The third example came from the Duna area in Papua New Guinea where a female native spirit who was thought to look after the environment was said to empower women or men by giving them healing powers consequent on experiences of possession trance. Trancing, then, is another classic mechanism whereby healers may be thought to attain their power, so that it is trance that produces the performative element in the ritual of shamanic healing.

Summing up, we identified in this paper three patterns of performativity: one through embodied mimesis, another through symbolic specialization and divination, and a third through trancing. In our second paper, we elaborated on these patterns, drawing more extensively on cross-cultural case materials, from Taiwan (Puyuma and Paiwan peoples), Papua New Guinea (Maring and Baruya). Elements we added to the earlier model of cases were: dreams, songs, visits to the world of the ancestors, the role of shamans in relation to fighting, inspired invocations of spirits and the protective powers of shamans against occult forces from outside of the group.

Performativity has recently been supplemented as a term in ritual analysis by 'efficacy'. Two issues of the *Journal of Ritual Studies* explored the issue of efficacy in detail. The seven empirical studies discussed in these two issues all dealt with ideas of spirit involvement in illness and healing, divination, possession, and bridges between ritual and mental health-care treatment. We pick out two contributions in particular along with Comments we ourselves made in the collections.

Johannes Quack and William S. Sax explored the general question of efficacy (Quack and Sax, 2010). These authors begin by posing the issues in conventional ways, that is, do rituals 'really' do what their performers claim they do? Answers were given by way of saying that rituals were 'really' about the expression of internal psychological sentiment, not about changing external processes in the world (p. 5) – which the observers probably did not believe to be possible, while they did wish to find that rituals achieved some aims or had some results. The word 'aims' is important here, because these aims may be complex. In a case study in the issue of the *Journal of Ritual Studies* (24, (1), 2010) an aim in funeral rituals among the Kyrgyz people is to obtain spiritual merit bestowed on by the dead. The writer of the study (Roland Hardenberg) translates this into 'renewing the socio-cosmic order'. The vocabulary is different here: one is the participants' indigenous view incorporating ideas about spirits, the other is the anthropologist's view, translating 'spirits' into 'order'. In functional terms these are the same. In epistemological or ontological terms they are quite different.

In their joint contribution Johannes Quack and Paul Töbelmann carry the interpretive conversation further (Quack and Töbelmann, 2010). They argue that we should abandon attempts to impose an 'instrumental' versus 'expressive' dichotomy on the analysis of rituals, because ritual acts combine both dimensions (p. 16). They also propose that a distinction should be made between 'effects' and 'efficacy'. Effects may be very broad, and go beyond the immediate or intended aims, whereas efficacy refers only to the intentions or functions of the ritual, from the viewpoint of either the practitioners or the observers (if the two are not the same). Efficacy may be the same for both practitioners and observer, but they may ascribe different causes; for example, a shaman's actions may be followed by a patient's recovery from an illness, which the shaman may attribute to the spirits whereas an observer may say it was because the patient's anxieties were allayed and they were no longer plagued by negative feelings or dreams and so on. Holding to the spirit of their definition of efficacy, Quack and Töbelmann distinguish their approach from that of Moore and Myerhoff (1977) who sought to differentiate doctrinal from operational efficacy (similarly to Rappaport's [1968] distinction between cognized and operational models). Operational efficacy, they point out, is simply a way of inserting the observer's viewpoint into discussion about the consequences of a ritual (p. 19). Quack and Töbelmann follow this up further with a sophisticated discussion of the arguments about ritual practice in the work of Catherine Bell. They point out (p. 22) that Bell's interpretations of the processes of ritualization mostly speak to issues of power and empowerment. They do this in two ways. First, Bell suggests that ritualization works to produce a particular set of perceptions, or misperceptions, about reality. Second it works further to produce and legitimize hierarchies of power in the society. In other words, we may add here, Bell's theory is functionalist, with a slight underlying Marxist twist. We will return to this conclusion later. However, we wish first to present the different theoretical thinking of Geoffrey Samuel in the same Special Issue of the *Journal of Ritual Studies*, Part 2 (2010). Samuel takes up the familiar topic of illness that is seen as a result of spirit attacks. Such a notion may be combined with other 'naturalistic' ideas of causation, but it adds to these the dimension of 'moral-ethical judgment' connected with the concept of spiritual agency, since spirits and people are in a moral relationship (Samuel, 2010, p. 8). Samuel seeks further to avoid the mind-body dichotomy that lies behind many interpretations of healing rituals. Observers have been willing to accept that rituals might affect a patient's mind, but not their body, whereas mind and body in fact go together, as argued by Thomas Csordas and his theory of 'somatic modes of attention' in healing (Csordas, 1997, p. 87, cited by Samuel; Samuel, 2010, p. 13). Introducing his idea of the 'body image', Samuel argues that healing works on this arena of experience, and that concepts of spirits or gods are ways of apprehending and dealing with states of the whole body system. Patients treated by Tibetan shamans, he proposes, integrate into themselves the narrative images of healing so that harmful beings are seen as extruded and beneficent ones are enabled to help. Still preserving to some extent an observer's viewpoint, since he does not appeal to 'occult forces' (p. 16), Samuel concludes that 'the language of spirits' is a means of 'providing tokens and images for operating on the structure of human life at all levels'; (p. 17). In sympathy with Samuel's conclusions, we ourselves in our comments on the papers in the *Journal of Ritual Studies*, (24), developed an idea of 'the moving walkway of analysis', which, we said, has to 'lead us across the mind-body dichotomy' (Strathern and Stewart, 2010b, p. 3, see 2010c).

Excursus: Bourdieu, Bell and misrecognition

Our discussions above have entered into the embattled arenas of ritual theorists arguing about how rituals 'work' or do not 'work'. We have seen that there is a persistent tendency to separate the views of the participants in a ritual from those of the analyst. We have also seen that successful attempts to find a middle ground of interpretation generally involve bringing closer the views on both sides, often with implications for breaking down mind-body dichotomies. We are going to take a reprise on these issues with a critical excursus on the work of two very famous theorists, Pierre Bourdieu and Catherine Bell, with special reference to the concept of misrecognition.

The noted French sociologist and ethnographer, Pierre Bourdieu, contributed greatly to embodiment theory in anthropology, for example, through his concepts of habitus and hexis (Bourdieu, 1977, s.v. in index of book, see also, LiPuma, Postone and Calhoun, 1993 for an appreciative critique of Bourdieu's work). These concepts in turn become relevant for ritual theory when juxtaposed with Catherine Bell's idea of ritualization and the ritualized body. (On embodiment and ritualization see our Introduction to this book.)

The concepts of Bourdieu and Bell can be helpfully applied across the whole spectrum of theorizing about ritual processes, see also Quack (2010). Bourdieu introduced another concept, that of misrecognition, which gives a further twist to this theory of ritual. One meaning of the term misrecognition as Bourdieu employs it appears to be intentional self-deception. When discussing the rituals of harvesting grain crops among the Kabyle people of Algeria, he notes the practices centred on the last sheaf of grain harvested from the field. He writes that these practices were based on an idea that the harvest is a kind of murder of the field which has been fecundated by ploughing (and sowing, surely) and is later 'stripped of the produce it has brought to maturity', (Bourdieu, 1977, p. 132). The last sheaf is given special ritual treatment because it contains the spirit of the field itself, Bourdieu says (p. 132), in a way similar to numerous instances garnered by Frazer in his *Golden Bough* (see Chapter 2 in this book, and Frazer, 1958, pp. 463–91 on corn spirits). The implicit murder of this sheaf is ritually transformed into an acceptable sacrifice, Bourdieu argues. Thus, the ritual produces an acceptable *misrecognition* of the harvesting act itself. The ritual is, according to this argument, a collective act of self-deception. Misrecognition, therefore, appears as a concept similar to the idea of mystification in Marxist theory (see, in general, Bloch, 1983), although not in the context of class-based domination. However, it is not clear from this example that any misrecognition of an objective reality takes place, because everything that happens in the harvesting ritual belongs to culturally created subjective meanings. If cutting the corn is seen as like a murder the harvesting ritual transforms this perception into a legitimate sacrifice, and this shift is recognized by the actors as a transformative sequence that the ritual – and only the ritual – can achieve.

Another classic ethnographic context in which Bourdieu situated his misrecognition idea is that of gift exchange, with critical echoes of the work of Marcel Mauss and Claude Lévi-Strauss (Bourdieu, 1977, pp. 5–6). Bourdieu criticizes what he portrays as the orthodox model of gift exchange, the idea of the reversibility of the gift (reciprocity in Lévi-Strauss's terms, obligation to return the gift in Mauss's terms). Bourdieu points instead to the importance to the normative idea of temporal delay between gift and counter-gift as well as to the contingency and variability of returns being made at all. He goes on to argue that 'the operation of gift exchange presupposes (individual and collective) misrecognition (*méconnaissance*) of the reality of the objective "mechanism" of the exchange, a reality which an immediate response brutally exposes' (p. 6). In this same passage he goes on: '[T]he lapse of time *separating* the gift from the counter-gift is what authorizes the deliberate oversight, the collectively maintained and approved self-deception without which symbolic exchange . . . could not operate. If the system is to work, the agents must not be entirely unaware of the truth of their exchanges, which is made explicit in the anthropologist's model, while at the same time they must refuse to know and above all to recognize it' (p. 6).

Bourdieu goes on further to develop his idea of practice as an art enacted in timed sequences rather than simply governed mechanically by norms. Here we are surely in the realm of conscious behaviour, for how can agency and strategy be unconscious? But before we consider this point, let us pause to consider two features of Bourdieu's formulation here. First, he ascribes an, albeit limited, degree of awareness of the 'truth' of exchanges to the actors. Such an idea seems to be in sharp contrast to an idea that misrecognition might imply a complete lack of consciousness of the supposedly objective social truth on the part of the actors. The second point here is to ask how true is it that the actors are only partially aware of the 'realities' underlying their action-sequences? Is it really necessary at all for them to deny the norm of reciprocity that in 'the anthropologist's model' (according to Bourdieu) is given the force of a social norm? The ethnographic scope of these two questions, as applied to Bourdieu's text, is a crucial issue here, because as Bourdieu goes on in this passage of his text (1977, pp. 5–7) he clearly switches to the Kabyle case, in which seemingly the code of honour implies an ethic of 'generosity', that is, that gifts are given without a specified notion of return – yet, of course, such returns are indeed generally made, and masters of the art of choosing when and how to make such returns gain 'symbolic capital' (or 'prestige') through doing so.

If now we extend the scope of enquiry into the ethics of gift exchange to the voluminous literature on the Pacific region, we may find a number of varying answers to the issues of consciousness and reciprocity raised above. For the Mount Hagen area of the Papua New Guinea Highlands, at least, the answers are clear when applied to the formal context of exchanges known as *moka* (see, e.g. A. J. Strathern, 2007, 2009; Strathern and Stewart, 2000; Stewart and Strathern, 2000): the actors unequivocally state the norm that defines *moka*: when a *moka* prestation is made, not only should there be a return gift later, but the return gift should exceed the initial one. When this is achieved, the giver acquires esteem and is said to have made *moka* by giving wealth 'on the back of' (*mbukl-öl*) the earlier gift they have received. If the return gift merely equals the original or opening one, this is said not to be *moka* at all, but something akin to swapping, trading, or buying (*mel rarop roromen*). Honour resides, then, in a sort of generosity, and this is explicitly formulated in the context of reciprocity plus increment. If this norm is not achieved, then the one who fails to achieve it incurs shame and a loss of symbolic capital and would not be considered a reliable partner for the future. As far as we can tell, there is no misrecognition involved in these processes at all.

Indeed, if we now turn to Bourdieu's text, it appears that exactly the same consequence of failure to live up to the strategies of gift-giving applies in practice among the Kabyle. A receiver is obliged to the giver until he has made returns, and if he fails to make these he can 'be accused of ingratitude and stand condemned by "what people say", which is what gives his actions their social meaning' (Bourdieu, 1977, p. 6). In substituting strategy for role and sense of honour for rules of honour, Bourdieu is surely placing the conscious actor squarely in focus, even if the actor is also instantiating the habitus, the underlying durable dispositions that guide the improvisations of action itself. Yet Bourdieu recoils from allowing the actor to be the explainer of his own actions, arguing that 'native theories are dangerous' because they may reinforce the intellectualist tendencies of academics to appeal to rules, and thus to the 'fallacies of the rule' (Bourdieu, 1977, pp. 19, 22). At this point, all we can comment is that neither actors nor anthropologists simply appeal to 'rules' in the way that Bourdieu maintains here: in short, he has reduced his opponents to 'straw persons'.

Later uses of the term misrecognition in the *Outline of a Theory of Practice* imply a greater emphasis on structure than is apparent from the earlier passages which we have examined above. Chapter 3 of the book deals with 'generative schemes and practical logic' (p. 96), and Bourdieu argues that practical logic, working through the habitus, reproduces systems of 'symbolic relations', that is, 'the oppositions and hierarchies which actually organize social groups and which they help to legitimate by presenting them in a misrecognizable form' (p. 97). Here, it seems, 'logic' is the 'agent' of action, rather than the strategizing and embodied actor. This reference to practical logic is mirrored later in Bourdieu's text by his use of the term 'practical taxonomies' (Bourdieu, 1977, p. 163). He writes: 'Practical taxonomies, which have a transformed, misrecognizable form of the real division of this social order, contribute to the reproduction of that order by producing objectively orchestrated practices adjusted to these divisions' (p. 163).

Bourdieu continues, in a slightly different, but related, vein: 'Every established order tends to produce (to very different degrees and with very different means) the naturalization of its own arbitrariness' (p. 164). He applies this to 'the taxonomies of the mythico-ritual systems', here bringing us to the Kabyle case again (p. 165). As we might expect by now, in Bourdieu's terms ritual activities contribute decisively to this 'naturalization'. We can see, therefore, how Bourdieu's ideas feed directly into ritual theory.

Here we see the by now familiar scheme of analysis in which the actors produce forms or patterns, which the observer is privileged to see as corresponding to 'realities' of the social order, although the actors themselves misrecognize the taxonomies as the reality itself. However, it is Bourdieu who is declaring that the actors misrecognize the phenomena, and we have to ask by what epistemological means he is able to do this, that is, exactly how he is able to know something that they do not know, what privileged access he has to objective (as opposed to the actors' objectified) 'reality'?

Finally, Bourdieu reveals more explicitly the relationship between his ideas and those of Marx:

Everything conspires to conceal the relationship between work and its production . . . Perhaps we should say that the relationship between work and its product is in reality not unknown but *socially repressed;* that the productivity of labour is so low that the peasant must refrain from counting his time, in order to preserve the meaningfulness of his work. (p. 176)

On the same page, Bourdieu refers to the 'indissolubly technical and ritual acts . . . such as fencing the fields, pruning the trees, protecting the new shoots from the animals . . . not to mention practices generally regarded as rites, such as actions intended to expel or transfer evil (*asifedh*) or celebrate the coming of spring' (p. 176).

Bourdieu sees these tasks as minor and unproductive in relation to the 'real' work of ploughing, sowing and so on. However, it is a purely speculative interpretation of the data to suggest that anything here is socially repressed, or concealed, or devised simply in order to preserve the meaningfulness of work because agricultural productivity is low. This, at least, looks very like an ethnocentric interpretation made from a capitalist-influenced viewpoint. In a broad sense, *all* of the actor's practices are 'productive', in the final analysis because they can be perceived as producing an entire adaptive way of life.

We now turn to the work of Catherine Bell.

Catherine Bell's concept of ritualization is akin to Bourdieu's general theory of the habitus. The ritualized body in Bell's usage may be seen as the exemplification of what Bourdieu meant by habitus in the embodied sense (see Bourdieu's concept, in this context, of the socially informed body, cited by Bell, 2009 [1992], p. 80). Bell adds the 'sense of ritual' to Bourdieu's reference to all the embodied senses, which include moral sensibilities as well as the 'sense of the sacred'. Bell notes that by this means (that is, adding a sense of ritual to Bourdieu's list) the generative capacities of ritual actions can be better appreciated and placed within practice theory (p. 80). She goes on to specify that practice is situational and strategic (pp. 81–82), then adds misrecognition as a third feature: 'The third feature intrinsic to practice is a fundamental misrecognition of its limits and constraints, and of the relationship between its ends and its means' (p. 82).

She explicitly traces the genealogy of the concept of misrecognition to its roots in Marx's work on practice, and supports it with reference to the same example of gift-exchange that we have critiqued above. It is important to note here that Bell simply accepts

Bourdieu's ideas and works them into her own approach. She does add a significant further element to the theory of practice, with her composite notion of 'redemptive hegemony', in which she attempts, boldly, to synthesize the ideas of two very different writers, the anthropologist Kenelm Burridge and the political theorist and activist Antonio Gramsci (Bell, 2009, p. 83); but we need not be concerned in detail with this idea here.

In a further sense, Bell's concern with empowerment leads her to assert that at the core of ritual is the creation and maintenance of power. In chapter 9 of *Ritual Theory, Ritual Practice,* she states that 'ritualization is first and foremost a strategy for the construction of certain types of power relationships effective within particular social organizations' (p. 197). She launches into a complex discussion of theories of power, at the end of it praising the French theorist Michel Foucault for regarding power as socially embedded and marked in people's bodies. All of this discourse goes back to Bourdieu's formulations of the embodiment and the objectification of power. However, it is notable that misrecognition does not figure strongly in this final chapter of Bell's book. The focus on ritualization itself does not need misrecognition as a part of its scheme, but it does crucially require the idea of the ritualized body. Bell's formulations here are ones that can be seen as entirely contemporary:

> Ritualization is fundamentally a way of doing things to trigger the perception that these practices are distinct and the associations that they engender are special. (p. 220)

And:

> Aside from the strategic and privileged distinctions established by ritualization, another primary way it acts is through a focus on the body . . . '. (p. 220)

At this point misrecognition is absent, while ritualization and the body are centrally in focus, fitting neatly enough with Bourdieu's habitus concept. A conjunction between Bourdieu and Bell is thus found, based on meaningful embodied action, at least momentarily bypassing misrecognition.

Critiques of Bourdieu's concept of misrecognition seem to be sparse in the literature. Many studies seem primarily to take the form of expositions, applications and minor recensions of his work in general, along with some thoughtful reconsiderations, (see, e.g. Calhoun, LiPuma and Postone, 1993; Brown and Szeman eds, 2000; Lane, 2000; Grenfell, 2004 and Rey, 2007). In her later book (Bell, 1997). Catherine Bell lays less stress on this concept than in her earlier one, which we have discussed here. One scholar in Religious Studies has produced a work on the ideas and embodied practices of the Manichaeans, organized distinctively around the ideas of the body held by the Manichaeans and their ritual practices (BeDuhn, 2000). BeDuhn delivers a trenchant critique of the misrecognition concept, in pursuit of his aim of trying to give an adequate representation of the Manichaean worldview. Eliding Bourdieu, he jumps straight to Bell, quoting from her earlier book, pp. 87–88, and concludes that according to her:

Native rationales are regarded as post hoc, arbitrary, and inessential. The universe that ritualists believe themselves to inhabit, and within which they act is, according to those who embrace this interpretive strategy, fictitious and illusory. (BeDuhn, 2000, p. 266)

Against this viewpoint BeDuhn argues that in order to explain why people perform a particular ritual, we cannot justifiably stand outside of their own sphere of discourse, because:

Ritualists respond to the situation they construe, and one cannot argue that they respond to a situation that is absent to them, one that has no means of eliciting their response. (p. 267)

He goes on:

None of the postulators of misrecognition provide an adequate mechanism by which an individual both perceives and does not perceive a situation at the same time. (p. 267)

BeDuhn's argument brings us to questions of cognition. Bourdieu's initial formulations provided a way out of this dilemma by suggesting that the actors are partially aware of the situation but adhere to what in effect is an ideological position that upholds the social status quo. Thus, it is not just cognition but rather discourse that is involved. Our own discussion has taken this argument further by arguing that in many cases the actors are actually well aware of what they are doing and there is no misrecognition at all, only a partial concealment at work. Thus, what they are doing would fit within BeDuhn's schema of the ritualists' own reasons for their actions.

Our suggestions here have been narrowly focused on one specific issue, namely that of misrecognition. All major theories in anthropology postulate interpretations that are conceptually independent of the actors' own statements, and the theories of Bourdieu and, following him, Bell have the great merit of being concentrated on the field of actual practice rather than on already reified abstractions. Granting this, however, our aim has been to introduce a note of caution into the process of theorizing, so that we do not leap over or ignore the interpretive insights and wider apprehensions of the people we work with: that we travel with them, following their lead, until we may wish to strike out in a direction of our own.

BeDuhn raises another philosophical perspective. He deploys the concept of 'subjected discourse', the subjective constructions of reality that people create through their lives. As with the Manichaeans, these subjected discourses change and are replaced over time. Old ones are rejected and new ones are adopted. However, he argues:

> Consider the inspired creation of human ingenuity they built upon what we take to be error. Consider the labor of love, of compassion, of universal human empathy they undertook, believing the world to be the sort of place where they could actually liberate the energies of life from pain, conflict, and death. (p. 271)

Aside from the point that 'reality' is always changing, the valuable point that BeDuhn is making is that ritual and religious practices can have complex and impressive purposes and values. The creation and expression of power may often be among these purposes or among the effects of ritual practices, but it is not necessarily the only matter that is involved. The world of ritual practice in fact encompasses the broad potentialities of the imagination and the reflexive ethics that people can create.

8

Cognitive approaches

Our discussion of 'misrecognition' as a concept in the previous chapter makes it clear that issues to do with cognition in general carry importance for ritual studies. Misrecognition implies a degree of error in perception, as judged by the observer. Cognitive studies of religion, centred on how the category of 'beliefs' comes into being, also overlap to some extent with questions of the performativity of ritual action. This is partly because it is precisely the supposed beliefs that motivate people's actions that analysts often point to as being 'illogical', 'mystical', 'irrational' and so on from their viewpoint, thereby raising the question of how and why these beliefs are upheld in action. Such assumptions are themselves based on a particular world view of what is possible or not possible in the world. At a deeper level, cognitive scientists attempt to map the lineaments of human cognitive processes, again to establish how people's thoughts, including their beliefs, are produced out of fundamental patterns of perception.

Since cognitivists have tended to approach ritual via the concepts of religion and belief rather than the other way around, we will begin here by looking at some attempts to theorize the cognitive wellsprings of religion. Such attempts carry an implicitly evolutionary content also, since they tend to hypothesize that the 'human mind' emerged as an adaptive phenomenon in the development of our species. The theories that cognitive scientists or psychologists invoke proceed from starting points closely similar to those of the nineteenth-century theorists such as E. B. Tylor with his notion of animism as the earliest form of religion; or the principle of the universality of the human psyche (= mind); or that the minimal definition of religion is the belief in supernatural beings (Tremlin, 2006, pp. 5–6). Tremlin translates 'supernatural beings' into 'gods' in this presentation, but we could cite ancestors or nature spirits as the equivalents in cognitive terms. Culture in this approach is also seen as the product of mental operations performed by the brain, which leads Tremlin to generalize that gods are ideas (p. 9), and ideas built on only a few fundamental patterns. Chapter 1 of Tremlin's book deals with the supposed prehistoric roots of 'the modern mind', a.k.a. 'intelligence' (Tremlin, p. 31). Intelligence here is essentially a social skill, enabling people to keep track of one another (ibid.), to understand that others have beliefs or desires (p. 32) and that, we might add, it is important to guess correctly enough what these are. Before proceeding here, we would like to note that the process of understanding others is partial and imperfect and can lead to errors, or difficulties, or conflict and aggression. Indeed, correct understandings can also lead to conflict, as when a person perceives that another is attempting to trick them, steal from them, or foist an untruth upon them (something that happens commonly enough in academic interactions between competing experts or departmental members). The Mount Hagen people of Papua New Guinea proverbially say that you cannot look into another person's mind (*noman*); although they also spend a great deal of time attempting to do just that (see Stewart and Strathen, 2001, pp. 113–37).

Tremlin moves to other themes regarding the mind, using the concept of mental modules, like computer software programs designed to carry out particular computational tasks, such as the postulated ability to acquire languages in Noam Chomsky's theory of universal grammar (see, e.g. Everett, 2012, pp. 73–102 for a critical view of this idea). Implicitly, in Tremlin's scheme, a centrally important module is 'the ability to quickly detect other agents in the environment' (p. 76). Tremlin suggests further that the capacity to distinguish 'agents' from 'objects' is important for survival. Cognitive scientists call this ADD, Agency Detection Device (p. 76). In order to work, they declare, it must be quick and focused, and by extension (this is crucial) able 'to make up agents based on minimal sense' inputs (p. 77). Errors can also be produced through misidentification,

Tremlin says (p. 77), and he moves on to note that ADD can 'over-attribute agency to objects' (ibid.).

At this point we must pause again. We can take note of the fact that agents and objects are distinguished differently in different cultures. Proverbially, in an 'animistic' lifeworld 'agency' is widely attributed to entities that might be considered 'objects' without sentience or intentionality. A great deal of ethnography has been written in this vein. Among hunter-gatherer populations of indigenous Australia, the whole cosmos was considered to be the living manifestation of ancestral agency from the 'Dreaming' time (e.g. Magowan, 2007). By the same logic, a volcanic stone among the Duna of Papua New Guinea could be seen as the petrified heart of an ancestor (Strathern and Stewart, 2004, pp. 59–60). Lawson and McCauley, two theorists of the origins of religion, suggest that humans have an 'action representation system' that tends to link actions to the activities of agents (Lawson and McCauley, 1990, cited in Tremlin, p. 78). This is a useful observation, but it fails to capture the complexity of ideas such as are implicit in the Duna example given above, where there is no immediate reason why stones should be interpreted as ancestors other than as a part of a complicated overall cosmology.

Tremlin also appeals to the concept of a psychologist, Justin Barrett, to effect that ADD becomes further specialized as HADD, Hypersensitive Agency Detection Device, a capacity that intrudes into many events, attributing agency to them (Tremlin, p. 78). Tremlin goes on to suggest that HADD is easily applied in domains where agency is already sensed, for example, in the identification of ghosts, because 'the idea of ghosts is ubiquitous the world over' (p. 79). Thus HADD plus the cultural idea of 'ghosts' produces narratives of spirit action. We must notice here that the concept of 'ghost' is introduced quite casually here as a simple fact that then feeds causally into the model of HADD, but might equally well be thought of as a product of HADD itself. In any case, from this kind of beginning, Tremlin suggests, came the proposition that gods (i.e. spirits, supernatural beings) are agents and have minds (p. 86). Given this, the next question is, how to influence them and why do people need to do so?

Tremlin reports on another turn in the cognitive argument, resting on work by Pascal Boyer (e.g. Boyer, 1990, 1994). This turn is an attempt to explain concepts such as 'ghosts'. Boyer sees such concepts as 'counterintuitive', because they go against 'natural expectations'. For example, when living creatures 'die', they are supposed to remain 'dead', but the notion of spirits or ghosts brings them linguistically back to life again. A problem here is that such concepts are already established or 'naturalized' in existing cultural contexts. In terms of cognitive processing, Tremlin suggests that counterintuitive concepts are built up from intuitive ones with certain elements removed or transformed. Animals that speak would be an example. As animals, they are easy to understand as existing, as language speakers they are not, but because they are animals the new counterintuitive idea that they can speak becomes believable (Tremlin, p. 90). As Tremlin notes, Pascal Boyer has made a grid of five ontological categories (persons, animals, plants, natural objects and artefacts) and three existential transformations that violate intuition, which is intended to cover all possible cases of counterintuitive processes (p. 93). Whether this is universally valid does not matter, because the list could be extended, but it is designed to provide an etic grid or calculus into which cases can be slotted, and so to provide a kind of universal grammar model of the production of ideas about spirits. What Tremlin, following Boyer, calls counterintuitive processes here is what Roy Wagner (1972, p. 160) called the innovation of meaning by the construction of metaphors, for example, 'on human mortality and the existence of ghosts'. By the same token a complex of metaphorical innovations of this kind would produce a set of beliefs. Beliefs, according to this model, are best understood as products of a neural net of ideas (see Tremlin, p. 138), some intuitive and some reflective, that is, a product of conscious discourse. Finally ideas about gods and spirits 'are attention grabbing, memorable, and highly portable' (Tremlin, p. 161), rather like wealth objects, we might say, and so come naturally to people (not so counterintuitive after all). In line with this argument is the view of Pascal Boyer that forms of divinations are an extension of ordinary processes of reasoning, enhanced by what he calls veracity guarantees (Boyer, 1990, pp. 68–72).

Harvey Whitehouse and his numerous collaborators have further developed the study of religion from a cognitive science viewpoint. The volume he co-edited with James Laidlaw carries a particular intellectual interest, because Laidlaw and Whitehouse disagree on the potentialities of cognitive approaches to the study of religion and culture, (Whitehouse and Laidlaw eds, 2007). Whitehouse considers that the potential of cognitive science to take over and explain the terrain of ethnographic facts is considerable, while Laidlaw expresses the opinion that such investigation can only explain the simplest elements and does not do justice to the complexities of cultural creations and of history. The realm that Laidlaw is concerned with is consciousness, and he argues that cognitive science tends to deal only with unconscious or semi-conscious processes of the mind (see Laidlaw, 2007, pp. 212–13 for a range of related considerations).

Whitehouse, by contrast, argues that, suitably extended into the world of conscious thought (what Tremlin calls reflective beliefs), cognitive science offers great potentiality for integrating ethnography and history together. He first notes (Whitehouse, 2007, p. 249) that 'explicit representations' are moulded by 'implicit cognition' (like deep structure influencing surface structure in some versions of linguistic theory). Since implicit cognition is general, this should mean that certain religious ideas will be widely found (ibid.). This, incidentally, returns us wholly to a Frazerian mode of investigation. Also, for particular cases, we would need to investigate how environmental conditions trigger or inhibit such general patterns. This implies micro-ethnographic work, and Whitehouse uses his own field materials from the Pomio Kivung movement in Papua New Guinea to illustrate how this can work out. He cites the emphasis on cleanliness, rigid adherence to rules, requirements to enter the temple one by one, and chiming a bell. Whitehouse explains all this by reference to a general cognitive mechanism called a 'hazard-precaution system', written about by Pascal Boyer (Boyer, 1994), who also distinguishes between proper (or 'real') threats to survival and the extension of the idea of threat into the domains of the sacred and taboo. (This again is like Wagner's metaphoric innovation.) To this we might, however, reply that the distinction represents the a priori imposition of an observer's world view on the ethnographic context. Whitehouse also sees in the Kivung rituals the workings of a HADD principle and the presence of moral values (p. 256). As he moves along in his analysis Whitehouse comes across the importance of analogies (= metaphors) in the religious representations of the Kivung (p. 265), and he refers to the theory that 'the capacity to make analogical connections between domain-specific forms of intelligence' (p. 266) is important in hominid evolution. This capacity is called CAT (cross-domain analogical thinking system). It may be said to provide a conscious and reflective element added to computational thinking. In our own Preface to the Whitehouse and Laidlaw volume, we illustrated structural features of the Female Spirit rituals in Mount Hagen to show agency detection, protection against danger of pollution, sense of order, and gender complementary (Strathern and Stewart, 2007, p. xv). Here 'structural features' all correspond to cognitive processes and the whole ritual could be described as a complex CAT grid. Missing, of course, from such an analysis is all the sociology and history of the practice, but cognitive theory is concerned with 'elementary structures' that can be built up into more complex models over time.

How do all these observations relate to performativity and efficacy? They do so in two ways: the performativity of a ritual will depend on how well it incorporates basic cognitive processes that appear to 'naturalize' it; and perceived efficacy will depend on the symbolic or cognitive construction of the ritual's elements. Camille Wingo has developed this theme by taking 'pictures' or 'images' as basic building blocks of ritual and exploring how they work as 'cognitive widgets' to shape a 'technology of ritual' that is seen as efficacious (Wingo, 2012, p. 79). This technology involves the creation of widgets (ritual shifters or elements) that mediate between percepts (objects of sense-perception) and concepts (meaningful items of thought). Items in rituals belong both to the perceptual and the conceptual world (i.e. they are symbols), thus creating a twofold reality. (A good example would be communion wine in Christian ritual as both wine and the blood of Christ.) Wingo also regards rituals as a kind of play, in which explicit propositions are avoided and iconic 'pictures' of action are made (as when the participants in the finale of the Female Spirit ritual dance out in decorated pairs). The items manipulated in this ritual (sacred stones, cooking ovens, ritual houses) all form what Wingo calls 'competence-based cultural objects' (p. 212). Examples from the Bemba girls' initiation rituals studied by Audrey Richards on which Wingo draws would be the special sculptures that have to be made to exact specifications and modelled on a *yongolo* type of snake (Wingo, pp. 211, 212). Wingo's exposition adds to those of Whitehouse the notion of a ritual widget (e.g. sculpture) which itself illustrates CAT processes of thought, since the sculpture of the snake both incorporates the image of a snake and stands at a more abstract level for manhood, an object of interest for the girls. Performativity therefore rests in the fit of this widget with the overall aims of the ritual. Wingo's contribution is to deepen the theory of how such widgets work. This is an action or practice-oriented theory in which 'beliefs', if produced, are a result rather than a cause of the actions undertaken in the ritual.

Beliefs, representations and enaction: The primacy of performance

Current debates about how to adequately understand or explain categories such as religion or ritual centre around whether we are primarily dealing with beliefs and representations about the world or with forms of embodied action engaged with, and in effect co-defining, the world. This division of viewpoints curiously replicates the reified distinctions that are sometimes made between 'mind' and 'body', and also much older anthropological debates on whether we should approach religion on an 'intellectualist' basis or a 'functionalist' (or sociological) perspective. Tylor's early work on animism as the primordial form of religion is often cited as the effective starting point of the 'intellectualist' approach. His central idea was that religion is based on a belief in spiritual beings and that these beings have their own agency separate from the bodies, including human bodies, that they may dwell in, and that they survive the physical death of those bodies. This seems like a complex set of metaphysical speculations. There is, however, another side to Tylor's ideas, which is not followed up by those who assign to him ancestral agency as the origin of the intellectualist theory of religion as 'belief'. That side is the experiential side, in which Tylor argued that people were concerned to understand what made the difference between 'a living body and a dead one' (Tylor, 1970: 12, originally published in 1871); further that they were interested in the phenomena of working, sleeping, trance and diseases, and also in what are the sources of the shapes that 'appear in dreams and visions?' (ibid.). These are not 'intellectualist' issues, they are ones that relate to embodied experiences and how people try to deal with them, obviously as emotional, existential and interpretive problems for sentient beings such as humans. So much, then, for any notion that Tylor's theory is purely intellectualist (or a form of disembodied cogito theory), even though he does refer to a putative set of 'ancient savage philosophers' (p. 12) Further, it has to be admitted that Tylor's general formulations are paralleled by innumerable ethnographic cases which seem to show dualities of classifications of the living and the dead (but not body and mind), and of the importance of dreams in revealing the wishes and concerns of ancestral kin.

Nurit Bird-David (1999) has, however, attempted a recension of Tylor's theory of animism in terms of a putative 'relational epistemology' that does not dichotomize body and spirit (1999, p. 568). Seeing Tylor's work as an instantiation of a modernist viewpoint foisted on ethnographic others, (see Bruno Latour, 2010, to be discussed later in the present chapter), Bird-David undertakes to excavate the truer meaning of animist concepts among the Nayaka, a tiny group of hunter-gatherers in South India (568). Using ideas derived from the work of J. Gibson and Tim Ingold, and appealing to an idea of dividual persons first promulgated for South India by McKim Marriott, she argues that *devaru* spirit entities are 'objectifications' of sharing relationships with the environment which the Nayaka practice. Human performers 'bring to life' (569) these *devaru* while in trance, joking, singing and sharing with them as they do with one another. Why this makes the *devaru* 'dividuals' is not entirely clear, other than that they are conceptualized as like human relational persons (a person can be relational without being dividual). What does seem to be at stake here is the definition of 'person'. In the English language, person implies 'human'. However, Meyer Fortes pointed out long ago that for the Tallensi people of Ghana a crocodile may be a person, if it is an incarnation of a lineage ancestor (Fortes, 1987, p. 249, originally dating to 1971). So we need a term that can bridge across from humans to non-humans or one that recognizes an occult potential aspect of one life form as concealing another. That is the first conceptual step needed to understand *devaru*. The second step is to see that the *devaru* also combine what is otherwise, again in English, separated as spirits (disembodied) and living humans (embodied). This bridging is accomplished performatively in the trance rituals in which humans come to embody the *devaru* in a manner that could indeed be described as sharing personhood. Bird-David herself stresses the aspects of relationality and sharing, derived from the Nayaka everyday performance of kinship relations and sharing, and she argues that the *devaru* 'objectify sharing relationships between Nayaka and other beings' (573), seen as kin. It seems, then, that the overall matrix of conceptualization is kinship, that kinship means sharing, and that hills and other parts of the environment are seen as kin with whom sharing can take place and from whom benefits can be obtained. This seems to mirror the actual Nayaka performances of practice, but it does not answer the question of why hills and other aspects of the environment are brought into the realm of kinship. That question can be answered by considering the ecological importance of hills and the processes of enskillment that allow people to enter into transactions with them. The relational epistemology involved must be one of generalized reciprocity and exchange, and the reason why people enter into these relations with their environment is that they consider the environment to consist of living beings and indeed 'superpersons', as Bird-David puts it, who can help humans. The concept of 'superpersons' is now added to the idea of kinship and appears itself to be a transform of 'supernatural'. In other words, the Nayaka create a cosmos of life that builds on human patterns and through the ideology of 'life' creates *devaru*. The Nayaka idea of stones that jump towards them indicating that they are *devaru* can be paralleled exactly from the lifeworld of the Hageners of Papua New Guinea and their concept of stones that are the Female Spirit and are then seated in special ritual houses for ritual activity. The stones are perceived as having agency as well as life and are thought of as the vehicles in which the Female Spirit wants to come to her human male worshippers (see Strathern and Stewart 1999a). This is not because the stones are 'dividuated persons'. It is because they have become the 'houses' of the Spirit, just as a human body may house a spirit and enable it to show itself.

The stones are not 'objectifications' of the Spirit, but they are simply the vehicles by means of which people recognize the coming of the Spirit to them. The Spirit takes their form, and so the stones also *are* the Spirit (not a 'representation' of her, either). It is the performance of 'finding' these stones, which also spontaneously 'come' to the males the Spirit chooses, that constitutes the relationship. The Spirit comes as a human bride comes to the settlement of her husband, she comes willingly and grants her powers to the husband. This is all realist 'performance', not 'objectification'. The idea of relatedness as the sole link between humans and 'spirits' is also, it might seem, rather insufficient to explain how the 'animist' idea of spirits could arise at all, so it cannot by itself replace the original speculations of Tylor. It is not, perhaps, so much that Tylor was wrong, but that he situated primitive philosophers in a *cogito* that was insufficiently ecological, in the sense that Ingold (e.g. Ingold, 2011) has given to this concept, of situatedness and openness in the world (a viewpoint which comes very close to phenomenology, but with an ecological emphasis).

In her overall assessment Bird-David moves away from cognitive science universalism into cultural relativism presented as a relational epistemology that is non-dualistic. Dualism and monism can to some extent coexist, but the quest for non-dualism is fuelled by dislike of the Cartesian mind/body/spirit (although it should be remembered that for Descartes the idea of the soul or *anima* was important as a *tertium quid* (see Strathern, 1996, pp. 42–45 on this point). Other writers have also exerted themselves in this arena of debate (see the discussions at the end of Bird-David's article).

Manuel Vásquez, in his extraordinary and broad-ranging book *More Than Belief* (Vásquez, 2011, 186 ff.), introduces his critique of the cognitivist work on religion by Harvey Whitehouse and others by noting how Whitehouse begins his own enquiries from the writings of Tylor. Vásquez also jumps at once from Tylor to the contemporary cognitivist work of Pascal Boyer, who has written about the 'naturalness' of religion (e.g. Boyer, 1994). Boyer's own viewpoint, like that of other cognitivits, is that what we call religion is an outgrowth from normal adaptive modes of operation in the environment in which people attempt to discern agency and intentionality in the things around them and in doing so anthropomorphize the sources of such agency (or rather personalize it, we might say). Other cognitive scientists (as we have noted earlier in this chapter) have dubbed this capacity ADD, and its outgrowth HADD. Since ADD and HADD are a part of the brain's ordinary operations, religion, if seen as a product of such cognitive mechanisms, 'appears as a natural outcome of the way in which our brain works' (Vásquez, 2011, p. 188). Religious notions, in turn, spread easily, because they posit agencies that are like natural ones but add a counterintuitive element, such as granting animals the power to speak. Religion is based on minimally counterintuitive concepts (MCI) (p. 189).

Vásquez is not concerned at this point to demolish all of this speculation about religion, but he does want to move on to a different viewpoint, which he calls 'religious enaction' (p. 195). The concept, along with his embrace of what he calls a proscriptive rather than a prescriptive evolutionary logic, enables him to see evolution as ruling out some behavioural patterns but allowing many others that are compatible with survival (p. 197). Such variable patterns of religion and ritual practices are what he calls religious enaction. This is not a new idea in itself, see for example, A. J. Strathern, 1996, pp. 181–90, and for updated theories of embodiment see Strathern and Stewart, 2011.

Vásquez critiques the cognitive theories of Whitehouse, Boyer and many others on two grounds. One is that religion is not a matter of belief but rather a matter of practice, a part of doings things in the world. This observation obviously fits well with the context of ritual, since ritual is by definition a kind of embodied performance, with intended or resultant performative efficacy. It cannot exclude the matters of belief or cognition entirely from consideration, since these are patently of great significance for some versions of what Whitehouse has called 'doctrinal religions', although it would be better to speak of faith, or doctrine itself, rather than belief in some instance. (Protestant values have tended to stress faith and sincerity of faith since the 'confessional' times in Europe, but these issues go far wider than the characteristics of Protestant Christianity; see also Seligman et al., 2008, and for a very thoughtful broad set of reviews of the relationship between ritual and belief, Harvey, 2005a, including the essay in it by Schieffelin, 2005.)

The second criticism that Vásquez makes is related to the first. He notes that religion and ritual have to do with the senses and relate to emotional experiences and the transformations of space, and in general to tactile-kinetic matters and to material and expressive culture (p. 199). This point is very like the points made in the volume co-edited with Whitehouse himself by James Laidlaw (Laidlaw, 2007).

According to Laidlaw's view, the cognitive theories so far proposed account for only the most elementary aspects of religion and ritual and so are by no means complete in their explanatory coverage. Laidlaw and Vásquez, are undoubtedly right here, and the rich arenas of ethnographic exposition of specific ritual systems clearly outrun the mechanical application of a few cognitive principles such as HADD and Theory of Mind (ToM). To each theory its own domain, however. These cognitive principles may correspond in generality to the earlier theories of Tylor and Frazer. They may help us to see why there are recurrent patterns in cases around the world. They will not be able to explain everything in themselves. Combined with other approaches, they may help us to achieve a more holistic set of understandings.

Vásquez further discusses the work of two other prominent theorists, Roy Rappaport and Tim Ingold and also work by James Gibson. He recognizes Rappaport's importance in the study of ecology and religion, and notes how Rappaport went further and suggested that religion and the idea of the sacred have 'played a key role in humanity's evolutionary adaptiveness' (p. 314). He criticizes Rappaport, however, for introducing 'the specter of functionalism', and for conveying 'heavy teleological assumptions' about self-regulation in systems (ibid.). (See also here some of our own, earlier, work, e.g. Strathern and Stewart, 2010d, reprinted from 1998, and 2001; also Senft and Basso, 2009, on 'ritual communication' generally. Our two works cited here dealt mostly with the details of Rappaport's work on the Maring people of Papua New Guinea. Rappaport's own complex and subtle reformulations in his last book prior to his death should be consulted – see Rappaport, 1999.)

Vásquez next turns to the work of the two further authors, James Gibson and Tim Ingold. Gibson, he says, emphasizes the ecology of perception, arguing that things in the world provide 'affordances' to ecological perceptions on the part of animals. This should be broadened to include all living things, such as plants, surely, because plants are also involved in constructing their worlds of interaction and reproduction. Vásquez is here partially following the work by Karen Barad on 'intra-action' by agents 'within a single material matrix of becoming' (Vásquez, p. 315). Barad advocates performativity over representationalism, and seeks to create models of agential configurations between living beings (Barad, 2003). In advocating performativity, she focuses on actions and their effects, while she links language to representationalism. Barad's interventions are obviously very incisive and important; however, two qualifying points may be suggested. One is that language itself is not just representational, but performative, as shown by the work of Austin, Hymes, Searle and many others on speech acts and ways of speaking as forms of action (see in general Duranti, 1997 on all these theorists). The second point is that setting human action into a broader context of ecology does not in itself constitute a 'post-humanist materialism' as Vásquez, following Barad, intimates, because in a wider sense it can help to create a finer humanism in which humans collaborate with, rather than dominating, an entity dubbed 'nature': ecological humanism, in effect.

Proceeding with his argument, Vásquez revisits the idea of the sacred, and suggests that it results from the affordances that places offer to 'the culturally in-skilled embodied schemas' by means of which these affordances are given salience (p. 318). This observation enables him to move on, and embrace, Tim Ingold's vision of an 'ecology of life' which is thoroughly embodied and attains holism through being non-dualistic, that is, does not split subject and object or nature and culture, matter and mind (p. 318). Embodiment and emplacement also go together (ibid.). We can only applaud this final Ingoldian analytical position, in large part because in terms of ritual theory it exhibits the best fit with the holism of experience that we constantly encounter in ritual events and their self-emplacement in the cosmos they create and by which they are created. The overall point here is not that these ideas totally negate the theories of the cognitivists, but that they situate those theories within a much broader, and, it can be argued, more powerful scheme of both understanding and explanation.

Several recent works tend to dovetail or partially complement the perspectives opened up in Vasquez's book. The emphasis on embodiment and emplacement in it is very much in line with much contemporary theorizing, including some of our own publications (again, see e.g. Strathern and Stewart, 2011). We would only caution that both 'body', and 'material' are terms with multiple meanings and connotations. The body in question is what Margaret Lock and

Nancy Scheper-Hughes long ago (1987) called 'the mindful body', and the term 'material' also carries a fan of connotations, including a suggestion of gesturing towards Marxist Theory, but Vasquez seems not to intend this, instead he wishes to gesture to a field of activity that focuses, as he says 'on the interplay of culture and nature, of neurophysiology, consciousness, practice, and history' (p. 110): certainly an inclusive view of materiality. (For a very concentrated view of this same arena, approached via the lens of archaeology, see Boivin, 2008, an important contribution to this brand of theorizing.)

We will mention here a series of works that overlap with Vásquez's synoptic vision. Philippe Descola and Gísli Pálsson's edited collection on 'Nature and Society' (1996a) followed innovatively a long line of questioning the distinction between nature and culture that seemingly underpins the thinking of major structuralist writers such as Descola's predecessor Claude Lévi-Strauss. Descola and Pálsson take up their stand against the dualism implied in an oppositional dichotomy between nature and culture by noting that it 'hinders true ecological understanding' (1996b, p. 3). Ingold in this same volume stresses social apprenticeship as the means whereby ecologically sensitive enskillment is obtained among hunter-gatherers, and urges that the ethnography of practice is the only way to understand what they do (Ingold, 1996). Descola points out that ecological study must be able to take into account facts such as that among the 'Tukanoan Indians of eastern Colombia, reciprocity is based on a principle of strict equivalence between humans and non-humans sharing the biosphere' (Descola, 1996, p. 89). Signe Howell, writing about the indigenous Chewong people of the Malaysian rainforest, notes that 'they do not set humans uniquely apart from other beings which they regard as sentient' (Howell, 1996 p. 128). And Edvard Hviding, drawing on his detailed work with the people of Marovo lagoon in the Solomon Islands, affirms a 'mutualist' rather than a 'dualist' view that holds among these people with regard to their ecological life patterns. He stresses their pragmatism. And he relates all this to patterns of emphasis on shared substance, production and consumption within territories characteristic of this part of Oceania, as depicted in A. Strathern's (1973) essay on Mount Hagen ideas from the central highlands of Papua New Guinea (Hviding, 1996, p. 173). All these studies take a pragmatic, anti-dualist, and ethno-oriented view of ecological agency, reflected also in their ritual and magical activities. They conform well also with Ingold's 'eco-practice' approach, if we may call it that. In the context of ritual theory such approaches converge on a performative view of ritual action, answering questions of what ritual does rather than what beliefs it is based on. The eco-practice approach is elegantly illustrated in Ingold's and Jo Lee Vergunst's edited collection on *Ways of Walking* (2008), with its obvious implications for pilgrimages (see Lund, 2008, in that volume).

A witty excursus on many of these themes is found in Bruno Latour's *On the Modern Cult of the Factish Gods* (2010). Latour is concerned to break down the same nature versus culture, subject versus object and body versus mind dichotomies that many others have critiqued. He does so in an original way, that in addition ironically reframes the issue of belief that we have seen appears to be part of an argument between cognitivists and practice theorists about how to understand ritual action. Latour points out how European colonists historically regarded indigenous religions as being based on erroneous beliefs, whereas they, the colonists, saw themselves as having true knowledge. We ourselves have earlier called this the problem of 'the epistemological switch' (Stewart and Strathern, 2002c, pp. 15–17). According to Latour, the colonists saw native practices as based on erroneous beliefs; but the people themselves, starting from different ontological premises, saw their practices as simple facts. For example, they made icons and these icons were also deities. This compressing of fact and idea together is what Latour calls the creation of 'factishes', valued facts which outsiders may interpret as 'fetishes' based on fantasy or error. Latour thus points out that it is the colonists who believe in belief, although they do not believe what they take to be the natives' beliefs. The indigenous peoples themselves are not bothered about belief because their ontological premises do not require it as a mental mechanism. Latour has a strong argument here. Ethnographically we can add to it by noting that there is always a ritual process of empowering and sacralizing icons, thus either transforming them into deities, or encouraging the deities to come and inhabit the icons as their house or dwelling place or seat; so it is ritual that bridges over from creation to worship. Possibly 'belief' is encoded in the ritual. More likely, the rituals act as 'widgets' to install the deities or ancestors in their proper places where they can be communicated with. In religious contexts that are paramount for Christian theology, of course, belief in the sense of faith and trust, as we have noted earlier in this chapter, can be of enormous significance; whereas in other religions and ritual systems it may be practically irrelevant. Belief as a valued notion emerges out of contested sites of practice and discourse, outside of the taken-for-granted, goes-without-saying *doxa* realm delineated by Bourdieu (Bourdieu, 1977, pp. 164–71). (Bourdieu provides a vital clue to the arguments about nature versus culture by pointing out in this passage that 'nature' never appears in the world of doxa; in other words the idea of nature is a product of an already differentiated and alienated mode of production according to this argument.)

Graham Harvey's Introduction to his valuable edited collection *Ritual and Religious Belief*, (Harvey, 2005b; see also David Hicks ed., *Ritual and Belief*, 2002), thoughtfully gives consideration to the interplay between ritual and belief, concluding that beliefs become significant when they are embodied in action, and also noting that in the past 'a considerable portion of academic writing about ritual has been skewed by a denigration of performance and a privileging of ideas (Harvey, Introduction, p. 3). Certainly; and yet closer inspection of Protestant religious practices will reveal that they enshrine numerous ritualizations of their own in accordance with the religious habitus that they create.

This remark brings us full circle in this chapter. Rituals do involve representations and certain ideas which might be described as beliefs may underlie these representations. But the representations are better conceptualized as ontological realities in themselves (factishes in Latour's terms). And ritual performances are enactions of cognitive processes that find their realities not in abstract ratiocinations but in embodied performative actions. Ritual is as ritual does. How extraordinary that the spirit of such a conclusion was anticipated long ago by a theoretician and ethnographer rarely remarked on nowadays, R .R. Marett, in his aphorism 'My own view is that savage religion is something not so much thought out as danced out' (Marett, 1914, p. xxxi). Strip the statement of what Latour might call its modernist stance, shown in the term 'savage', and you have a theory of ritual as peformative action and of ritual 'in its own right' (in the terms of Handelman and Lindquist, 2005).

9

Conclusions: Framings and values

Camille Wingo's book has the title *Pictures Making Beliefs*. In this short conclusion to our book we will discuss how rituals construct values through framing. The image of a 'picture' will form a 'widget' in our argument here, that is, assist with the argument.

Pictures contain an image within a frame. The frame does not define the subject of a picture in terms of its content, but it does place a boundary around it, and the character of the frame itself blends with the picture. If we see now the frame as frames of a moving picture we begin to get an idea of how a ritual process works. For a ritual the very first notion of framing would be one that conveyed the sense of 'This is a ritual'. However, since such framings can vary greatly in their intensity or explicit character, one theorist interested in embodiment and practice approaches to ritual, Catherine Bell, wrote of ritualization, the process in which a ritualized body is produced as a foreground against a background of other forms of action (Bell, 1997). Special clothing is one obvious example, the spatialization of action another (classically studied by J. Z Smith, 1987, and comparable with a large anthropological literature on places and landscapes, see, e.g. Feld and Basso eds, 1986; Stewart and Strathern eds, 2003). All contextual delimitations and forms of the direction of attention can be described as framings. Framings may also be placed around a certain kind of action in order to signify that the meaning is not what it might appear to be, as with Gregory

Bateson's famous work on framings in the Iatmul *naven* ritual of achievement in Papua New Guinea (Bateson, 1958). For example, an act of apparent violence may receive a framing that announces it is not serious, or that the meaning is the opposite. A friendly act can be converted into an act of hostility, as in the Pangia area of the Southern Highlands of Papua New Guinea when a presentation of pork, normally considered a mark of friendship, is seen as hostile when the pig is butchered in a different way (*poi mokora*) (Strathern and Stewart, 1999b). An apparently hostile act can be given a friendly meaning when a male celebrant in Mount Hagen charges up and down a row of tethered pigs to be given away in a *moka* exchange with ex-enemies in warfare, brandishing a spear and twirling an axe (Strathern, 2007 and www.StewartStrathern.pitt.edu/papua_new_guinea/photogallery/set-I.html). Framing therefore crucially influences a ritual performance and its performativity in creating either enmity or amity. (For revisions and subtleties surrounding this issue see the *Journal of Ritual Studies*, 26, (2), 2012 with contributions by Michael Houseman; Steven Engler and Mark Q. Gardiner; Eddy Plasquy; Jens Kreinath and Don Handelman.)

In this book we have reviewed some salient approaches to the analysis of ritual actions, beginning from nineteenth-century theorists steeped in the Classics and European folklore, and proceeding through the changes wrought by writers such as Radcliffe-Brown, Claude Lévi-Strauss, Meyer Fortes and Victor Turner (from structure to process to drama). We continued with a general enquiry into the topic of sacrifice, and then with special themes such as ritual failures, ritual secrecy, performance and perfomativity and cognition. One main division in ritual studies is that between the aim of presenting indigenous action in its own terms (the 'Ritual in its own Right' approach of Handelman) and the aim of presenting outside explanations or interpretations of ritual, for example, by showing how rituals create or are created by social values at large. The first approach can be termed internalist, the second externalist. In most synthetic forms of theorizing it is desirable to bring these two approaches together in pursuit of a more holistic and dynamic understanding. One problem with our initial image (or 'widget') in this chapter is that the concepts of frame and picture are static, not capable of encompassing the immense dynamic forces that are often unleashed in ritual activities. We therefore need at least a concept of both frame and picture changing over time in the enactment of a ritual performance. Indeed, a similar comment can be made about many of the cognitive approaches we have outlined in the previous chapter. Cognitive capacities are seen as mental phenomena, and therefore to some extent they re-instantiate Cartesian-style mind-body dichotomies that embodiment theory (innovatively brought into the mainstream of theory by Thomas Csordas in a set of significant publications e.g. Csordas, 2002, 2009) has sought earnestly to transcend. Ritual performances very often involve elaborate embodied activities, such as the feet-stamping final dance of the Female Spirit rituals in Mount Hagen, Papua New Guinea which is extremely energetic and requires advance practices to enable the performers to endure it and do it well (Strathern and Stewart, 1999a and www. StewartStrathern.pitt.edu/papua_new_guinea/ritual_and_social_life. html). Theories to explain or understand this aspect of the Female Spirit syndrome must therefore take into account the importance of this kind of dynamic movement of dancing. Why must the performers dance in this way? People say that the dancing shakes the earth and that it resembles thunder in its sound, remarks that indicate an association between the Spirit and severe weather or earth tremors: a metaphor for powers of the environment or *kona* ('place').

With these points in mind, we return to our image of the picture and its frame. Frame here is what defines, indicates, or suggests that a ritualized embodied process is entered into and exited from. In trying to decide what ritual, or a ritual performance, actually 'is', theorists have appealed to the idea that there can be degrees of ritualization of action: in Catherine Bell's terms, the production of ritualized bodies (e.g. dancers) leads to ritual actions that are stereotyped, declared to be traditional, formalistic, invariant, naturalized and rule-governed (Bell, 1997, pp. 138–69). There can therefore be differences in the degrees to which such features are realized in practice or are transformed. In any case, what finally determines that an event or process will be marked out in a special way is that it receives a frame. There is a point at which this frame is announced or comes into play, either by a verbal statement or by a gesture or the ringing of a bell, anything that punctuates time and space and creates a new beginning or a recursive return to an earlier event. As Jonathan Z. Smith eloquently put it: 'Ritual is a relationship between "nows" – the now of everyday life and the now of ritual place; the simultaneity but not the coexistence of "here" and "there"' (Smith, 1987, p. 110). Ritual may be said also to create an enhanced 'now-time' of experience that separates it off from other aspects of 'now' (see Strathern and Stewart, 2009, p. 7, referring to Pentecostal Christian practices in Papua New Guinea). Now-time has to be constructed through special framing, which may involve music, song and the cognitive preparation of people via 'somatic modes of attention' in the terms developed by Csordas (Csordas, 2002, pp. 241–59). Such modes of attention do not occur spontaneously, but are led up to through special embodied ritualizations. The mode of consciousness and attention generated thus becomes a second frame within the general frame of, say, a church service or a healing ritual. Framing focuses attention and leads to cognitive and affective results. Framing thus in effect not only defines a ritual space but also influences what happens 'in the picture' that the frame encloses.

We turn at this point, however, to the second part of the analysis: what is in the picture? This question is directed to the old problem of meaning in rituals (or any social action). We suggest here that what is in the picture is a portrait, albeit indirect, of important values for the society or the group and so on. Such an elementary idea is obviously in line with very old lines of thinking about ritual, as found in Frazer's 'Psyche's Task' or the work of Radcliffe-Brown on kinship, taboo, joking relationships and totemism (Radcliffe-Brown, 1965). The argument made here, however, is not that rituals express social values but rather that they are instrumental in making them, bringing them about. Initiations do not express a value of gendered maturity, they create that value within the ritual.

This brings us back to the issue of ritual efficacy. Why should the task of creating values in these ways fall to ritual activity? An answer to this part of the problem would have at least to take into account the idea that rituals provide (a) a unique context of 'reality', and (b) this appears in images that are striking and memorable, or (c) are repeated sufficiently often for the memory of them to influence the ritualized body. (These categories correspond to the significant work of Harvey Whitehouse on types of memory and ritual experience, see, e.g. Whitehouse and Laidlaw eds, 2004.) Embodiment theory has to be fed into a model of this kind because it is bodily displays that make the effects we are discussing here. The heightened sense of reality is provided by the framing of the event and the character of the symbols presented in it that connect with general cultural experience (see Barth, 1987 on Baktaman initiatory symbols). The ritual frame may also serve to increase the affective level of the performance. The values that are encapsulated in ritual actions should not necessarily be expected to be discursive, although explicit discursive elements may enter the scene. They are rather, as we have said, images, with multiple associations (multi-vocalic in Turner's terms). Their effects are aesthetic. They must appeal to some cognitive domain that does not need to be translated into propositional language (or even into 'semi-propositional representations', in the phrase of Dan Sperber, 1985). This does not mean that they have to appeal to some amorphous unconscious domain of the mind. Indeed, they may be effective at the conscious level also, but for their effects they have to operate subliminally.

Dimitris Xygalatas has tackled this kind of question of analysis in his book on fire-walking rituals of the Anastenaria in Agia Eleni, northern Greece (Xygalatas, 2012). After describing in detail the customs themselves, this author embarks on an extended exegesis of their cognitive underpinnings. (He set out to study the Anastenaria as himself a Greek but not one who knew the village itself, and he initially contrasted his position with that of Loring Danforth who had worked on the same topic in Agia [Ayia] Eleni from 1973 to 1976 and subsequently and published a monograph on it centred on 'religious healing' in 1989.)

Xygalatas begins his analysis by facing the same question that we have posed above: why rituals? (p. 125). He assents to the notion that many rituals are puzzling to 'the observer' (who?) because they are non-rational and cannot have the results they aim to achieve. He likens rituals to obsessive-compulsive forms of individual behaviour (p. 126). But rituals are collective and normative, not individual or seen as pathological. He next asks why costly rituals? Anastenaria takes a great deal of energy and endurance, and Xygalatas goes to Costly Signaling Theory for his explanation here, and describes costly religious ritual as a hard-to-fake signal (p. 133) of general commitment to group ends. This is plausible, but one has to ask who is measuring the cost when the participants actually enjoy the event itself? This issue comes up when

Xygalatas next deals with arousal and motivation. The Greek church holds rituals that are repetitive and monotonous, with little potential for arousal, he argues, thus placing them into one of Whitehouse's two categories of religious action or 'modes of religiosity', the doctrinal mode as distinct from the imagistic mode (Laidlaw, 2004, p. 4). The Anastenaria, by strong contrast, is local, experiential and imagistic, and provides an alternative mode of transmission of values and creation of memories from the doctrinal mode of the church. The two modes can be seen as 'attractors' (Xygalatas, p. 150) that create different sorts of memories and attachments and stimulate participants over time to offer exegetical reflections on why they take part in the rituals in question, especially for the high-arousal rituals such as fire-walking. Once exegesis is established, it reinforces commitment and transmission of the ritual itself (p. 165). Xygalatas recognizes the importance of physiological sensations here, so his cognitivism extends to include embodiment; and he concedes, perhaps a little reluctantly, that 'the practice of high-arousal rituals can have some actual therapeutic results' (p. 179), and that in any case high levels of collective action are in themselves rewarding for the participants (what we might call 'the we did it' principle) – something that Durkheim and the structural-functionalists would not have failed to recognize, with or without cognitive science. Danforth, in his study (1989, pp. 84–131) devotes a whole chapter called 'From Illness and Suffering to Health and Joy', taking into account the importance of the Saints Constantine and Helen as figureheads of miraculous victory against odds – surely an iconic image for fighting and overcoming illnesses of many kinds? Danforth further points to the importance of songs, myth and metaphors as rhetorical operators in the healing process, noting that central to the therapeutic transformation 'is an elaborate set of metaphors of emergence, release, and opening up' (Danforth, 1989, p. 122). Danforth's study thus clearly belongs to the same lines of interpretation of healing delineated with precision by Csordas (e.g. Csordas, 2002 on Navaho healing). Danforth also finds no need to appeal to obsessive-compulsive behaviour as an explanation. Our own finding here is that, as Whitehouse has argued, cognitive and other forms of explanation can be combined and made into more powerful models, but cognitive science is not a substitute for imaginative, aesthetic and culturally sensitive investigation. Danforth was the 'outside' investigator, and Xygalatas the 'inside', yet here their roles appear to have been reversed. Perhaps Danforth identified more easily with a tiny peripheralized village of 400 people in the north of Greece (in the Malinowskian mode, we might say), whereas Xygalatas tells us (p. 4) that he grew up in a busy urban centre of about a million people. As an urban cosmopolite, he might be expected, perhaps, to feel more 'different' from the people of Agia Eleni than if he himself had grown up among them. When his informants told him that they did the Anastenaria 'for the Saint(s)' (p. 153), this was perhaps the most profound reason they could have given. The Saint holds all the powers of healing and history. The ritual contract is to honour the Saint by taking the icon which participates in sacred power – its materialization – on a ritual journey and walking through fire as the Saint himself did. The Saint is the portrait in the picture, notionally carried as an icon across the fire, and in that image lies the power of healing. That is the value the ritual upholds and the value of the ritual. Similar analyses can be applied to the ethnography of shamans and shamanism (see, e.g. Balzer, 2011 for a fine example).

Having discussed the question of frames and values, we want to end this book by suggesting that the most powerful pathway to the understanding and explanation of rituals is to combine embodiment theory with cognitive theory, bringing together, in a sense, the ideas of Thomas Csordas and others on embodiment (see, e.g. Strathern and Stewart, 2011) with the ideas of Harvey Whitehouse and his many collaborators (e.g. Whitehouse and Laidlaw eds, 2007) on cognition. An author whose works continually repay close attention in this regard is Maurice Bloch, who adds also another element that we consider to be vital, the relationship between language and cognition. The issue cannot be considered as settled: language and cognition go together, but cognition can occur without linguistic vocalization. Bloch has also consistently sought to bring together cognitive and cultural factors in his own ethnographic analyses (see, e.g. Bloch, 1998, 2005). What we need from now on is a systematic effort to find grounded theory that would allow us to set cognitive science and cultural or sociopolitical analysis onto a single plane of explanatory work in the study of ritual, as well as in other contexts of social action.

Appendix 1

Temple renewal rituals on Jinmen island, Taiwan

The two Jinmen (or Kinmen) islands lie offshore by only about two kilometres from the city of Xiamen, belonging to the People's Republic of China (PRC). The Jinmen islands belong politically to the Republic of China (ROC) in Taiwan, where Chiang Kai-shek's forces retreated in 1949 after losing control to Communist forces. Although Jinmen is far from the main island of Taiwan, the ROC forces successfully held on to it after 1949 and large numbers of Taiwanese military forces were stationed there. The United States supported the position of the ROC in Taiwan and helped to protect Jinmen, although the PRC forces continued to intermittently bomb it until late in the 1970s (Szonyi, 2007, pp. 185–86, 2008). Local society was under strong military control, and Jinmen was in the forefront of the global Cold War for a long time, and in particular of the struggle between Taiwan and the PRC.

The situation today on Jinmen is quite transformed. In the past it had been enclaved away from the mainland of Taiwan and equally from the PRC, a political, historical and cultural isolate, with its own local dialect Jinmanese. It is all the more remarkable that today, with the opening up of travel between Taiwan and Fujian Province in the PRC and with Jinmen as the conduit through which this travel passes, the island has become a venue for tourists and the old sites that commemorated the 'heroic resistance' of ROC forces to the assaults by the PRC military are now made the objects of heritage, while Jinmen is linked more and more to the outside world in general.

In December 17–21, 2010, we were privileged to be able to record a remarkable process on the main Jinmen island of renewal for a village ancestral temple that is a focus for ritual activity on the part of a leading local group (the Ong or Wang lineage) and its affinally linked families or lineages.

The renewal ritual was one that is needed periodically to update and/or replace ancestral tablets (memorials for the dead) and to give a place to certain living successors in the families of the lineage so that they would eventually, after death, be enshrined in the temple building. These temple buildings are elaborately decorated and furnished with all kinds of ritual insignia. Refurbishing the tablets and the roof beams ritually installed with octagonal endings for good fortune and many other features caused considerable expense. We were able to make records and images of the temple because a graduate student from the National Tsing-Hua University's Anthropology Department kindly invited us to come from Taipei and stay in the house of her aunt (her mother's sister) and took us to the temple site and to many other such sites including the shrine to Wang Yulan on Lieyu (Little Jinmen) island (see Szonyi, 2007 for an account of the Wang Yulan story). Through her we gained access to the temple and to the meanings of the many ritual practices that were performed within it. The temple stood only a few minutes away from where we were staying, and our visit further coincided with the December winter solstice or seasonal change rituals that involve household heads in presenting pink and white sticky rice balls and other special foods to the shrines of household ancestors on the top floors of houses, together with the lighting of candles, burning of incense, and burning of paper currency for the dead, all as markers of respect and means of petitioning for health and good fortune in the ensuing months. These domestic rites coincided with some continuing festivities at the village temple.

Temple rites of the kind that we learned about on this visit are elaborate performative exercises that integrate together the concerns for well-being of all the local households that worship in the temple because the tablets of their lineage forebears are established within the temple's structure. The temple building is expensive to renew and therefore demonstrates the financial standing of the constituent households and especially of prominent males within these. The temple is also a site which protects against bad or hostile energy (*sha-qi*) and which is itself so protected by the placement of special bricks at its corners. The temple structure lends itself to the kind of sociological analysis known in the past as structural-functionalist associated with the work of A. R. Radcliffe-Brown (e.g. Radcliffe-Brown, 1965). This is because it is through such structures that the major lines of social identification, integration, hierarchy, wealth and gender relations are affirmed and strengthened. This point is obviously true for the present case. However, at the levels of the cultural meanings and senses of cosmic emplacement in time and space much more can be learned from considering some of the details of the temple's renewal.

We were told that much preparatory ritual had taken place in the two months before our research visit. We also were told that it had been 40 years since the lineage tablets had last been renewed and rededicated, and also that lineage daughters of the village married elsewhere would have to wait another 12 years if they were unable to attend this time and take part. In general, one of the interesting features of the whole ritual complex related to the place in it of female lineage members and of the ties of marriage and affinity created through them, including some aspects in which women were granted rights of participation on an innovatory basis.

The time depth of 40 years since the last renewal of the temple is interesting because it would coincide with what Szonyi remarks on as the campaign of the ruling Guomindang party in the ROC to foster a campaign on behalf of national consciousness, to be accessed through tradition. As Szonyi points out, 'because of its front-line position, Jinmen had a distinctive role to play' (2007, p. 189). Chiang Kai-shek, in fact, had advocated the principle of religious freedom as against the Communists' opposition to all forms of religion, including ancestor worship, so the reconsecration of a local temple would certainly have been favoured at that time.

Many Jinmen people today prefer to regard themselves primarily as Jinmenese (rather than solely Taiwanese) and are also proud of the depth of their genealogical ties sometimes tracing them back more than 20 generations to various parts of the Mainland of China from which their remote forebears supposedly came. They contrast themselves doubly both with Taiwanese who live in the island of Taiwan itself, saying that they do not know their own genealogies because they were often cut off from that knowledge when they migrated to Taiwan, and with Chinese mainlanders, who until recently were not permitted to practice popular religion because of government policies against religion generally. In some sense, therefore, they see themselves as unique custodians of tradition, preserved precisely because of their former isolation and enclavement in a military and cultural outpost. Their perceptions of their cultural roots in the Mainland, via Xiamen, are strong, and it was noticeable in the accounts of the ritual materials that were procured for the temple renovations that the renewed ancestral tablets were actually made by craftsmen from Fujian Province in the Mainland, rather than locally. The reason given was that the price from the Mainland was only half that charged by locals; but there was also a sense that the workmanship and the knowledge behind it was better and that the tablets would be coming from the old ancestral land and therefore carried ritual precedence (see, for a parallel, the case of temple materials in the Penghu Islands, Stewart and Strathern, 2007, p. 11). For the 2013 temple renewal, guests came from Putian in Fujian, and there were altogether some 50 lineage guests from elsewhere in the Mainland of China generally, as well as some from Tainan in south-west Taiwan where the Minnan language of Fujian is spoken and the people also practice worship of the goddess Mazu, who is said to have come from the Mainland (see Stewart and Strathern, 2007, pp. 4–9). Jinmen rituals look both inwards in an intensely local way, and outwards to east and west.

The actual rituals performed at the site were all geared to establishing the perceived correct alignment of the building itself and its parts, of the hierarchy of social relationships in the village, and of the timing of events in accordance with the birth-date zodiac positions of worshippers. Performers also played drums slowly in order to mark the beginning of the ritual drama, which was designed to drive away the effects of negative qi or harmful ghosts, while within the temple assemblages of elders, and the chairman of the whole ritual process, would watch over presentations of foods such as rice dumplings offered to the ancestors. Certain people's birthdays were said to be opposed to their taking part in the rituals at certain hours on those days, and hence they stayed away; but otherwise specific men were responsible for acts of worship, such as those directed to the Earth God. The chairman of the whole event mostly had the duty of expressing and leading the worship to the ancestors. Household representatives had to walk round a display of nine bowls of rice dumplings and three bowls containing gold-coloured paper money used in burning as offerings (odd numbers are auspicious). Women were active as greeters of guests. Various sections had tasks, such as lighting firecrackers. Special honour was paid to participants who were successful professionals, such as a doctor, or a general or someone with a PhD degree. Such professionals were asked to pay donations for the event because the idea was that their success was in part a blessing from the ancestors and they should make suitable returns of thanks to the ancestors for this blessing. Some concessions were apparently made to females throughout the whole event. For example, one man's daughter who has a PhD degree was permitted to hang up an inscribed board in the temple, a role otherwise played only by males. Here the daughter's educational status took precedence over her gender.

Kinship relations were prominent throughout. The whole genealogical calculus of the Ong lineage was displayed in tablets. Another lineage, Yang lineage, played a prominent part in acts of worship because of long-established relations of intermarriage with female natal Ong lineage members. The Yang lineage members live in a different part of the area but their ancestors long ago had given help to the West Dinbao people (the temple owners) to build the first temple. Various kinds of temples were also important ritual venues for local marriages. A couple intending to marry had first to visit their ancestral temple to worship their ancestors and later had to sacrifice a pig and sheep and dedicate these to the Sky God at a different folk temple. Married daughters returning for temple rituals are expected to pay a sum of New Taiwanese Dollars 200 (approximately equal to $6.50) to purchase chopsticks inscribed with their names and used to consume the ritual foods.

One piece of material culture used in the rituals is of particular interest. Containers for candle lights were placed before the ancestral tablets. These special containers are named after the Big Dipper seven star constellation, and this ritual was designed to draw the energy of the constellation into the tablets in accordance with the local version of Daoism. In the past only agnatic lineal descendants were allowed to carry these tablets, but on this occasion cognates (males related to the lineage through females) were also able to carry the tablets. A Daoist ritual master asked the males holding the tablets of dead kin to blow on them to make a physical connection with the tablets and ensure that the energy of ancestral qi would be passed down to male descendants over generations and to ensure prosperity. The importance of continuity and the wealth needed to ensure it is underscored here, as well as the underlying significance of qi as a concept. A further detail graphically illustrates the significance of continuity of descendants. One man was elected to open the gateway into the temple. This man had to be someone all of whose children and nephews had sons, in others words a kind of super-grandfather. His descendants must not be divorced. He himself had to have a healthy wife. He also had to choose an auspicious date to open the gate.

Two other ritual sequences are particularly worthy of note. One is an action of the visiting affines. Under the table with their offerings on it, they placed a bowl with a special plant, the *maosha*, in it. This plant is said to have a root that holds onto the land, that is, it also fosters continuity. If this is a cordyline plant, it would parallel the significance of cordylines in Highlands Papua New Guinea (see, e.g. Rappaport, 1968). The second ritual is that of 'crossing the cloth bridge'. This is a rite of passage and of purification. Participants passed over a cloth in the temple and had a red seal marked on their backs. Menstruating females, however, could not cross the bridge, although they could touch paper money. This rite indicates the limitations placed on female participation. The idea of the cloth bridge has to do with crossing over a threshold of misfortune or danger into a new year of prosperity. The aim of protection is also present. The same notion of protection seems to be embodied in the action that the universal or hyper-grandfather, the gate-opener in the ritual, (called *liugongquan*), had to undertake by walking around the whole village boundary to welcome the elders of the lineage. He and his whole family had to undertake this walk, and they had to perform it in the opposite direction taken by visiting affines (descent versus affinity).

A further point of the ritual was to link the temple with external sources of power. Males whose birthdays placed them in the dragon zodiac were led by the Daoist priest in performing the *zhui-long* drama of 'chasing the dragon'. They brought a representation of the dragon into the village to imbue the temple with its power. The head of the dragon was said to be at the source of a river on the peak of a prominent local mountain. The dragon's spine or its veins (*long-mai*) are said to connect the village to the source of the water and so to have the power to connect the mountain's qi, or energy of blessing, with the village. *Long-mai* is a conduit or a 'line of power'. One participant, of the Yang lineage, said that the local *long-mai* is actually an extension from a mountain in Fujian Province on the Mainland, Mount Wu Yi. This is an example of a 'ritual trackway', a pathway across landscapes linking diverse places together by means of the precedence of an original powerful place. The *long-mai* idea thus connects Jinmen to Fujian. Links with the Mainland were further constituted by the fact that the theatre group hired to perform during the ritual came from Quanzhou city, also in Fujian.

In summary, the ritual processes involved in reconsecrating the temple brought all households together, reaffirmed the power of cosmological symbols, established the temple in ritual (generational) time and geomantic space, concentrated the flow of good qi and warded off bad qi, demonstrated the wealth of prominent persons and all in all acted as a huge complex of divination in order both to access the blessings of the ancestors and to ascertain whether these blessings would continue in future, sealing each sequence with signals that both aims were achieved and secured.

Note

We wish to give especial thanks to Ms. Kuang-ting Chuang (and her family) for hosting us, for taking us to this and other temples, for explaining the many rituals, for sharing with us her DVD materials of the rituals, and for following up with further correspondence. Kuang-ting further worked on numerous occasions with Mr Shih-Hsiang Sung in Taipei to help classify further the complex and fascinating details of this extraordinary ritual event. Many thanks, therefore, also to Shih-Hsiang for his technical assistance with these materials, as well as our appreciative thanks to Kuang-ting for the unique field experience in Jinmen.

Appendix 2

The anthropology of disasters and disaster rituals

Disasters tax and challenge human social patterns and adaptations, thus revealing cracks and tensions in the social structure and demanding creativity in people's responses to these. In our ongoing project on this theme, we are examining the roles that rituals can play in such processes of adaptation. Ritual theory would predict that such roles would be considerable. Ritual is essentially a bridging practice, designed to move people from one social situation to another. Ritual also captures and channels people's emotions into pathways that enable them to cope with senses of anomie and disruption in their lives. Disasters often involve injuries and deaths in large numbers, and this in turn creates grief, stress, and a need to multiply the funeral rituals that accompany each death. Further, people lead lives that are emplaced within their surroundings and when these surroundings are damaged or impaired, such as with landslides or river floods, they experience a tremendous sense of wishing to re-establish themselves, and rituals of re-emplacement can be a very valuable way of achieving such an end.

We will take here just a few examples of the processes referred to above.

1   In 2009 in southern Taiwan, in territories of the Paiwan people (Austronesian speakers) Typhoon Morakot caused extensive damage in mountain areas, with landslides and massive changes of the riverbeds owing to the discharge of rocks and timber into the water and its chaotic outflow in lower areas. Paiwan families had to abandon their old riverside settlements and accept government and NGO schemes of resettlement in flatland valley areas without nearby access to farming land, and in housing quite different from their own established dwellings. One of the issues that emerged out of this obviously traumatic set of events was what to do with ritual practices. Christianity has long been well established in most Paiwan settlements, but questions and concerns regarding their earlier forms of religious practices remain. In the mountain villages there were ancestral shrines in which sacrifices would be made from time to time to important village ancestors, and leading families of chiefly status would look after these shrines unless they had converted to the new religion. In one village of the western Paiwan the old ancestor shrine was left in a part of the village not destroyed by the flooding of the nearby river, and there was no one clearly in charge of it. At an earlier time, Japanese authorities who governed Taiwan from 1895 to 1945 had required the villagers to move downhill from a still higher and less accessible area up in the mountains, and at that time the ritual specialists and authorities had been able to 'call' the ancestral spirits to come to the new area and be re-established there. With the 2009 relocation such a process of ritual transplacement became moot. 'Modern' relocation areas had no place for ancestor shrines. Instead room was made for the construction of various Christian churches, in accordance with the denominational adherence of subgroups to one kind of church or another. Some adherents of the old religion declined to be relocated, at least for the time being, partly because of their concerns for the ancestral shrine. Because of the new religious and ritual divisions and the split locations of the village subgroups, arguments further arose as to what the cause of the disaster had been. Christians argued that it was because some of the people had thought to revive parts of the pre-Christian rituals for performances designed also to be viewed by tourists, and that in practicing one of these performances a ritual mistake had occurred, and the performance had been viewed as undertaken seriously rather than as a purely commodified form. As a result, they said God had sent the floodwater as a punishment. The non-Christian ritualists, however, had an opposite narrative. They said that the flood had resulted from the anger of the ancestors because their rituals of worship were abandoned or neglected. Ritual dilemmas were thus set up, which were proving difficult to resolve.

2   In the eastern Paiwan area south of Taitung city Typhoon Morakot similarly caused massive disruptions. Relocation houses for Paiwan villagers were built in various locations, and at the time of our first field visit there in 2010 these houses were spoken of as being temporary or in temporary locations. Here the problems in some places were that people felt nervous and concerned in these new settlement sites: first, because the land was not theirs; second, because different groups were all brought together in an unfamiliar way; and third, because many people had died as a result of the typhoon and not all of the bodies had been found and given a proper burial. This last was a serious consideration because the ghosts of these dead people, both Han (Chinese) and indigenous (Paiwan and other named tribes), were considered to be dangerous and unsettled. As such, people felt that these ghosts might attack them, and that they needed to set up a ritual to show the ghosts a way out of a corner in the village plaza where they felt (probably via divination practices) that these ghosts had originally come in. The houses had been built by a Christian missionary organization (World Vision) and its officers did not consider they could agree to what they regarded as a pagan rite being performed. For the people, however, as in all such cases,

the problem was existential: the ghosts were there and needed to be expelled, otherwise they would cause trouble. Indigenous and Han notions came together here since in both cultures unhappy ghosts (known in Han practice as 'hungry', lacking in shrines where descendants could make sacrifices to them) are thought to bring with them sickness and misfortune. Here, then, was another situation of a ritual dilemma.

3   Over in the south-eastern parts of Taiwan, in the region of the city of Tainan, landslides from Typhoon Morakot in certain areas were so severe that in one case they engulfed most of a village of indigenous Plains aborigines (Pingpu Siraya), whose bodies were buried in the avalanche of mud and rocks. Their mourning relatives could not recover the bodies and thus were unable to determine how to locate shrines for them or how to communicate with their spirits. Shamanistic specialists stepped forward to handle the situation, running communal séance sessions for relatives of the dead to talk with the spirits, find out where they were and help to escort them to a place of quietude and rest, away from the disaster site. These specialists, belonging to popular forms of the Daoist religion with which the Pingpu are familiar, offered a timely ritual solution for an untimely disaster, taking on a psychopompal role and also gathering the souls of the dead so that they did not become hungry ghosts.

4   Christian churches often play important ritual venues or means of mobilizing people to help in occasions of natural disasters. In June 2012 we visited Western Samoa, a Pacific Island formerly governed by New Zealand until 1962 when it gained Independence, in order to learn about responses to a unique tsunami that had struck the southern coasts of the island in 2009 (the same year as Typhoon Morakot hit southern Taiwan). There was no historical precedent for such a tsunami in Samoa, we were told. Christian churches have been strongly established in Samoa for a long time and villages are organized around their churches and their *fale* or meeting houses. At the time the tsunami hit, churches were

among the first responders with aid, so their parishioners were mobilized as providers of help to those suffering and in need. At one village site we also saw a small shrine to a statue of the Virgin Mary which people said had been left miraculously standing while all the buildings around it were destroyed. Such a shrine can form a focal point for a renewal of ritual practices of piety. Church buildings themselves convey ritual significance. In central Taiwan, in Nantou Province, we visited a reconstruction and rehabilitation site that had been established following a devastating earthquake in the vicinity of the city of Puli, and there we found that a 'paper church' had been set up, a present from Kobe in Japan where a tsunami took place in 1996. An architect had designed the church earlier as a symbol of recovery for Kobe, and later the Kobe people packed up the church and sent it as a sign of compassion to the Nantou people in Taiwan. In a sequel in 2012, a massive series of earthquakes laid waste to large areas of the city of Christchurch in the South Island of New Zealand, irrevocably damaging the large Anglican cathedral at the city's centre. The people of Christchurch were distraught and upset when they learned the cathedral was beyond repair. The same Japanese architect who had built the paper church in Nantou then designed a paper cathedral to be sent to the people in Christchurch as a ritual consolation for the loss of their previous cathedral. (The paper in question, of course, was very strong and reinforced, but could be covered by a canopy.)

Bibliography and further reading

[This is a list of works cited in our book plus additional references relating to the topic as a further reference guide to our Readers.]

Ackerman, Robert (1987), *J. G. Frazer: His Life and Work*. Cambridge: Cambridge University Press.

Adler, Jeremy and Richard Fardon, eds (1999), *Franz Baermann Steiner. Selected Writings. Volume 1: Taboo, Truth, and Religion*. Methodology and History in Anthropology Volume 2. New York and Oxford: Berghahn Books.

Ahern, Emily M. (1979), 'The problem of efficacy: strong and weak illocutionary acts'. *Man,* (N.S.), 14, 1–17.

Austin, J. L. (1962), *How to Do Things with Words*. Oxford, UK: Oxford University Press.

Balzer, Marjorie Mandelstam (2011), *Shamans, Spirituality and Cultural Revitalization. Explorations in Siberia and Beyond*. New York: Palgrave Macmillan.

Barad, Karen (2003), 'Posthumanist performativity: toward an understanding of how matter comes to matter'. *Signs: Journal of Women in Culture and Society* 28, (3), 801–31.

Barringer, Judith M. (2008), *Art, Myth, and Ritual in Classical Greece*. Cambridge: Cambridge University Press.

Barth, Fredrik (1975), *Ritual and Knowledge among the Baktaman of New Guinea*. Oslo: Universitetsforlaget.

— (1987), *Cosmologies in the Making: A Generative Approach to Cultural Variation in Inner New Guinea*. Cambridge: Cambridge University Press.

Bateson, Gregory (1958), *Naven* (2nd edn). Harford, CT: Stanford University Press.

BeDuhn, Jason David (2000), *The Manichaean Body In Discipline and Ritual*. Baltimore: The Johns Hopkins University Press.

Bell, Catherine (1992), *Ritual Theory, Ritual Practice*. New York: Oxford University Press.

— (1997), *Ritual: Perspectives and Dimensions*. New York: Oxford University Press.

— (2006), 'Embodiment', in J. Kreinath, J. Snoek and M. Stausberg (eds), *Theorizing Rituals: Issues, Topics, Approaches, Concepts*. Leiden and Boston: Brill, pp. 533–43.

— ed. (2007), *Teaching Ritual*. Oxford and New York: Oxford University Press.

— (2009) [1992], *Ritual Theory, Ritual Practice*. Oxford, UK: Oxford University Press.

Besnier, Niko (1995), *Literacy, Emotion, and Authority. Reading and Writing on a Polynesian Atoll*. Cambridge: Cambridge University Press.

Bielo, James S. (2009), *Words upon the Word: An Ethnography of Evangelical Group Bible Study*. New York and London: New York University Press.

Bird-David, Nurit (1999), '"Animism" Revisited. Personhood, environment, and relational epistemology'. *Current Anthropology* 40, Supplement, 567–91.

Blenkinsopp, Joseph (1983), *A History of Prophecy in Israel. From the Settlement in the Land to the Hellenistic Period*. Philadelphia: The Westminster Press.

Bloch, Maurice (1983), *Marxism and Anthropology*. Oxford, UK: Oxford University Press.

— (1989), *Ritual, History and Power: Selected Papers in Anthropology*. London School of Economics Monographs on Social Anthropology No. 58, Michael Sallnow (ed.), London and Atlantic Highlands, NJ: The Athlone Press.

Bloch, Maurice, E. F. (1998), *How We Think They Think: Anthropological Approaches to Cognition, Memory, and Literacy*. Boulder, CO: Westview Press.

Bloch, Maurice (2005), *Essays on Cultural Transmission*. L.S.E. Monographs on Social Anthropology no. 75. Oxford: Berg.

Boas, Franz (1966), *Kwakiutl Ethnography*. Helen Codere (ed.). (Classics in Anthropology, Paul Bohannan, ed.). Chicago: The University of Chicago Press.

Bohak, Gideon (2008), *Ancient Jewish Magic. A History*. Cambridge and New York: Cambridge University Press.

Boivin, Nicole (2008), *Material Cultures, Material Minds. The Impact of Things on Human Thought, Society, and Evolution*. Cambridge: Cambridge University Press.

Bokenkamp, Stephen R. (2009), *Ancestors and Anxiety: Daoism and the Birth of Rebirth in China*. Berkeley, LA and London: University of California Press.

Boretz, Avron (2011), *Gods, Ghosts, and Gangsters. Ritual Violence, Martial Arts, and Masculinity on the Margins of Chinese Society*. Honolulu: University of Hawai'i Press.

Bourdieu, Pierre (1977), *Outline of a Theory of Practice*. Cambridge, UK: Cambridge University Press.

— (1990), *The Logic of Practice*. Richard Price (trans.). Cambridge: Polity Press.

Boyer, Pascal (1990), *Tradition as Truth and Communication. A Cognitive Description of Traditional Discourse*. Cambridge: Cambridge University Press.

— (1994), *The Naturalness of Religious Ideas: A Cognitive Theory of Religion*. Berkeley: University of California Press.

Brown, Nicholas and Imre Szeman, eds (2000), *Pierre Bourdieu. Fieldwork in Culture*. Lanham: Rowman and Littlefield.

Buc, Philippe (2001), *The Dangers of Ritual: Between Early Medieval Texts and Social Scientific Theory*. Princeton and Oxford: Princeton University Press.

Burkert, Walter (2001), *Savage Energies: Lessons of Myth and Ritual in Ancient Greece*. Peter Bing (trans.). Chicago: The University of Chicago Press.

Buss, Johanna (2007), 'The sixteenth Pinda as a hidden insurance against ritual failure', in U. Hüsken (ed.), *When Rituals Go Wrong*. Leiden: Brill, pp. 161–82.

Calhoun, Craig, Edward LiPuma and Moishe Postone, eds (1993), *Bourdieu: Critical Perspectives*. Chicago: The University of Chicago Press.

Carpentier, Martha C. (1994), 'Jane Ellen Harrison and the ritual theory'. *Journal of Ritual Studies* 8, (1), 11–26.

Chaniotis, Angelos, Silke Leopold, Hendrik Schulze et al., eds (2010), *Body, Performance, Agency, and Experience*. Ritual Dynamics and the Science of Ritual, Volume 2. Wiesbaden: Harrassowitz Verlag.

Clack, Brian R. (2004), 'Scapegoat rituals in Wittgensteinian perspective', in Kevin Schilbrack (ed.), *Thinking Through Rituals: Philosophical Perspectives*. New York and London: Routledge, pp. 97–112.

Clothey, Fred W. (2006), *Ritualizing on the Boundaries: Continuity and Innovation in the Tamil Diaspora*. Columbia, SC: University of South Carolina Press.

Cochrane, Laura L. (2013) *Weaving Through Islam in Senegal*. Durham, NC: Carolina Academic Press.

Codere, Helen (1950), *Fighting with Property. A Study of Kwakiutl Potlatching and Warfare 1792–1930* (Monographs of the American Ethnological Society, Marian W. Smith (ed.), no. xviii.). New York: J.J. Augustin Publisher.

— (1966), 'Introduction', in F. Boas, *Kwakiutl Ethnography*. Chicago: The University of Chicago Press.

Cook, Arthur Bernard (1915), *Zeus*. Cambridge: Cambridge University Press.

Cornford, Frances M. (1914), *The Origins of Attic Comedy*. London: E. Arnold.

Coulanges, Numa Denis Fustel de (n.d.), *The Ancient city,*Willard Small (trans.), first published 1873. Garden City, New York: Doubleday Anchor.

Crahay, Roland (1974), 'La bouche de la vérité: Grèce', in Remo Guidieri (ed.), *Divination et Rationalité*. Paris: Editions du Seuil, pp. 201–19.

Crossley, Nick (2004), 'Ritual, body technique, and (inter)subjectivity', in Kevin Schilbrack (ed.), *Thinking Through Rituals: Philosophical Perspectives*. New York and London: Routledge, pp. 31–51.

Csapo, Eric and Margaret C. Miller, eds (2007), *The Origins of Theater in Ancient Greece and Beyond. From Ritual to Drama*. Cambridge: Cambridge University Press. (General Introduction by Csapo and Miller, pp. 1–40.)

Csordas, Thomas J. (1997), *The Sacred Self: A Cultural Phenomenology of Charismatic Healing*. Berkeley: University of California Press.

— (2002), *Body / Meaning / Healing*. New York: Palgrave Macmillan.

— ed. (2009), *Transnational Transcendence: Essays on Religion and Globalization*. Berkeley, Los Angeles and London: University of California Press.

Danforth, Loring M. (1989), *Firewalking and Religious Healing. The Anastenaria of Greece and the American Firewalking Movement*. Princeton: Princeton University Press.

DeBernardi, Jean (2004), *Rites of Belonging: Memory, Modernity, and Identity in a Malaysian Chinese Community*. Stanford, CA: Stanford University Press.

Descola, Philippe (1996), 'Constructing natures: symbolic ecology and social practice', in P. Descola and G. Pálsson (eds), *Nature and Society: Anthropological Perspectives*. London and New York: Routledge, pp. 82–102.

Descola, Philippe and Gíssli Pálsson, eds (1996a), *Nature and Society: Anthropological Perspectives*. London and New York: Routledge.

— (1996b), 'Introduction', in P. Descola and G. Pálsson (eds), *Nature and Society: Anthropological Perspectives*. London and New York: Routledge, pp. 1–21.

Dharampal-Frick, Gita, Robert Langer and Nils Holger Petersen, eds (2010), *Transfer and Spaces*. Ritual Dynamics and the Science of Ritual, Volume 5. Wiesbaden: Harrassowitz Verlag.

Dodds, E. R. (1951), *The Greeks and the Irrational*. Berkeley and Los Angeles: University of California Press.

Douglas, Mary (1966), *Purity and Danger: An Analysis of Concepts of Pollution*. New York, NY: Praeger.

— (1970), *Natural Symbols: Explorations in Cosmology*. New York: Pantheon Books.

— (1975) [1993 reprint], *Implicit Meanings: Essays in Anthropology*. London and New York: Routledge.

— (1999), *Leviticus as Literature*. Oxford, UK: Oxford University Press.

Du Boulay, Juliet (2009), *Cosmos, Life, and Liturgy in a Greek Orthodox Village*. Limni, Evia, Greece: Denise Harvey Publisher.

Dumézil, Georges (1996), *Archaic Roman Religion*, vols. 1 & 2, trans. by Philip Krapp, with a foreword by Mircea Eliade. Baltimore and London: Johns Hopkins University Press.

Duranti, Alessandro (1997), *Linguistic Anthropology*. Cambridge: Cambridge University Press.

— ed. (2001), *Linguistic Anthropology: A Reader*. Oxford: Blackwell Publishing.

— (2009), 'Universal and culture-specific properties of greetings', in A. Duranti (ed.), *Linguistic Anthropology: A Reader* (2nd edn). Oxford, UK: Wiley-Blackwell Ltd., pp. 188–213.

Durkheim, Emile (1965), *The Elementary Forms of the Religious Life*. J. W. Swain (trans.). New York: The Free Press. (First published in French in 1915.)

Edmonds, Radcliffe G. III, ed. (2011), *The 'Orphic' Gold Tablets and Greek Religion*. Cambridge: Cambridge University Press.

Eibl-Eibesfeldt, I. (1970), *Ethnology: The Biology of Behavior*. New York: Holt, Rinehart and Winston.

Elliot, Alan J. A. (1955) [1990], 'The theory and practice of spirit mediumship', in A. J. A. Elliot, *Chinese Spirit-Medium Cults in Singapore*. London School of Economics Monographs on Social Anthropology No.14. London & Atlantic Highlands, NJ: The Athlone Press, pp. 46–79.

Evans-Pritchard, Edward E. (1937), *Witchcraft, Oracles and Magic among the Azande*. Oxford: The Clarendon Press.

— (1956), *Nuer Religion*. New York and Oxford: Oxford University Press.

Everett, Daniel L. (2012), *Language, The Cultural Tool*. New York: Vintage Books.

Falco, Raphael (2010), *Charisma and Myth*. London and New York: Continuum.

Feld, Steven and Keith H. Basso, eds (1986), *Senses of Place*. Santa Fe: School of American Research Press.

Fernandez, James W. (2004), 'Contemporary carnival (carnaval) in Asturias: visual figuration as a "ritual" of parodic release and democratic revitalization', in J. Kreinath, C. Hartung and A. Deschner (eds), *The Dynamics of Changing Rituals: The Transformation of*

Religious Rituals within Their Social and Cultural Context. Toronto
Studies in Religion Vol. 29. New York, Washington, D.C./Baltimore,
Bern, Frankfurt am Main, Berlin, Brussels, Vienna and Oxford: Peter
Lang, pp. 21–40.

Firth, Raymond (1973), *Symbols: Public and Private*. London: George
Allen & Unwin, Ltd.

Fortes, Meyer (1983), *Oedipus and Job in West African Religion*.
Cambridge: Cambridge University Press.

— (1987), *Religion, Morality and the Person: Essays on Tallensi
Religion*. Jack Goody (ed.). Cambridge: Cambridge University Press.

Frankel, Stephen (1986), *The Huli Response to Illness*. Cambridge:
Cambridge University Press.

Frazer, Sir James G. (1922), 'Preface', in B. Malinowski, *Argonauts of
the Western Pacific*. London: Routledge and Kegan Paul (republished
by E.P. Dutton and Co. 1950), pp. vii–xiv.

— (1927), *The Devil's Advocate*. 2nd edition of *Psyche's Task*; and *The
Scope of Social Anthropology*. London: Macmillan and Co.

— (1958), *The Golden Bough*, abridged edition in one volume. New York:
The Macmillan Company, sixth printing (originally published in
abridgement 1922 by Macmillan).

Friedson, Steven M. (2009), *Remains of Ritual: Northern Gods in a
Southern Land*. Chicago and London: The University of Chicago
Press.

Furley, William D. (2004), 'Athens and Delos in the fifth century B.C.E.:
ritual in a world of shifting allegiances', in J. Kreinath, C. Hartung
and A. Deschner (eds), *The Dynamics of Changing Rituals: The
Transformation of Religious Rituals within Their Social and Cultural
Context*. Toronto Studies in Religion Vol. 29. New York, Washington,
D.C./Baltimore, Bern, Frankfurt am Main, Berlin, Brussels, Vienna
and Oxford: Peter Lang, pp. 179–90.

Gardner, Don S. (1983), 'Performativity in ritual: the Mianmin case'.
Man (N.S.) 18, 346–60.

Gell, Alfred (1992), *Metamorphosis of the Cassowaries: Umeda
Society, Language and Ritual*. L.S.E. Monographs no. 51. London:
The Athlone Press.

Gennep, Arnold van (1960), *The Rites of Passage*, trans. by Monika
B. Vizedom and Gabrielle L. Caffee, with an Introduction by Solon
T. Kimball. London: Routledge and Kegan Paul. (First published in
French in 1908.)

Girard, René (1977), *Violence and the Sacred*. Patrick Gregory (trans.).
Baltimore: The Johns Hopkins University Press.

Glasse, Robert M. (1995), 'Time bilong Mbingi: religious syncretism
and the pacification of the Huli', in A. Biersack (ed.), *Papuan
Borderlands*. Ann Arbor: University of Michigan Press, pp. 57–86.

Goffman, Erving (1967), *Interaction Ritual: Essays on Face-to-Face Behavior.* Garden City, NY: Anchor Books.

Goody, Jack, ed. (1973), *The Character of Kinship.* London and New York: Cambridge University Press.

— (1977), *The Domestication of the Savage Mind.* Cambridge: Cambridge University Press.

— (2000), *The Power of the Written Tradition.* Washington and London: Smithsonian Institution Press.

— (2010), *Myth, Ritual, and the Oral.* Cambridge: Cambridge University Press.

Graves, Robert (1960), *The Greek Myths*, vols. 1 and 2, revised ed. London: Penguin Books.

Grenfell, Michael (2004), *Pierre Bourdieu. Agent Provocateur.* London and New York: Continuum.

Grimes, Ronald L. (1996), 'Ritual criticism and infelicitous performance', in R. Grimes (ed.), *Readings in Ritual Studies.* New Jersey: Prentice-Hall Inc, pp. 279–92.

— ed. (1996), *Readings in Ritual Studies.* Upper Saddle River, NJ: Prentice Hall.

— (2002), *Deeply into the Bone.* Berkeley: University of California Press.

Grosse, Christian (2008), *Les Rituels de la Cène: Le culte eucharistique réformé à Genève (XVIe-XVIIe siècles).* Genève: Librairie Droz S.A.

Halpern, Paul (2000), *The Pursuit of Destiny: A History of Prediction.* Cambridge, MA: Perseus Publishing.

Handelman, Don (2004), 'Re-framing ritual', in J. Kreinath, C. Hartung and A. Deschner (eds), *The Dynamics of Changing Rituals: The Transformation of Religious Rituals within Their Social and Cultural Context.* Toronto Studies in Religion Vol. 29. New York, Washington, D.C./Baltimore, Bern, Frankfurt am Main, Berlin, Brussels, Vienna and Oxford: Peter Lang, pp. 9–20.

— (2005), 'Introduction: Why ritual in its own right? How so?', in D. Handelman and G. Lindquist (eds), *Ritual in Its Own Right.* New York and Oxford: Berghahn Books, pp. 1–32.

Handelman, Don and Galina Lindquist, eds (2004), *Ritual in Its own Right: Exploring the Dynamics of Transformation.* New York and Oxford: Berghahn Books.

— eds (2005), *Ritual in Its Own Right.* New York and Oxford: Berghahn Books (pbk edn).

Hardenberg, Roland (2010), 'How to overcome death? The efficacy of funeral rituals in Kyrgyzstan'. *Journal of Ritual Studies* 24, (1), 29–44.

Harrison, Jane Ellen (n.d.), *The Religion of Ancient Greece.* Chicago: The Open Court Publishing Company.

— (1951), *Ancient Art and Ritual.* New York: Greenwood Press. (Earlier published 1913 in The Home University Library, London: Williams and Norgate).

— (1955), *Prolegomena to the Study of Greek Religion.* New York: Meridian Books (originally published in 1903, Cambridge: Cambridge University Press).

Harvey, Graham, ed. (2005a), *Ritual and Religious Belief: A Reader.* London and New York: Routledge.

— (2005b), 'Introduction', in Graham, Harvey (ed.), *Ritual and Religious Belief: A Reader.* London and New York: Routledge, pp. 1–16.

Heidle, Alexandra and Jan A. M. Snoek, eds (2008), *Women's Agency and Rituals in Mixed and Female Masonic Orders.* Leiden and Boston: Brill.

Henn, Alexander and Klaus-Peter Koepping, eds (2008), *Rituals in an Unstable World: Contingency, Hybridity, Embodiment.* Frankfurt am Main, Berlin, Bern, Bruxelles, New York, Oxford, Wien: Peter Lang.

Hertz, Robert (1960), 'The pre-eminence of the right hand: a study in religious polarity', in *Death, and the Right Hand*, Rodney and Claudia Needham (trans.). London: Cohen and West (originally published 1907).

Hicks, David, ed. (2002), *Ritual and Belief: Readings in the Anthropology of Religion* (2nd edn). New York: McGraw Hill.

Hillis, Ken (2009), *Online a Lot of the Time: Ritual, Fetish, Sign.* Durham, NC and London: Duke University Press.

Hinde, Robert A., ed. (1972), *Non-Verbal Communication.* Cambridge: Cambridge University Press.

— (1987), *Individuals, Relationship and Culture.* Cambridge, UK: Cambridge University Press.

Hobart, Angela (2003), *Healing Performances of Bali: Between Darkness and Light.* New York and Oxford: Berghahn Books.

Hobsbawm, Eric and Terence Ranger, eds (1983), *The Invention of Tradition.* Cambridge, UK: Cambridge University Press.

Højbjerg, Christian K. (2007), *Resisting State Iconoclasm among the Loma of Guinea.* Durham, NC: Carolina Academic Press.

Holbraad, Martin (2012), *Truth in Motion. The Recursive Anthropology of Cuban Divination.* Chicago: The University of Chicago Press.

Houseman, Michael (2006), 'Relationality', in J. Kreinath, J. Snoek and M. Stausberg (eds), *Theorizing Rituals: Issues, Topics, Approaches, Concepts.* Leiden and Boston: Brill, pp. 413–28.

Howell, Signe (1996), 'Nature in culture or culture in nature? Chewong ideas of "humans" and other species', in P. Descola and G. Pálsson (eds), *Nature and Society: Anthropological Perspectives.* London and New York: Routledge, pp. 127–44.

Hubert, Henri and Marcel Mauss (1964), *Sacrifice: Its Nature and Functions*, W. D. Hall (trans.), Foreword by E. E. Evans-Pritchard. Chicago: The University of Chicago Press (originally published 1899).

Hüsken, Ute, ed. (2007), *When Rituals Go Wrong: Mistakes, Failures, and the Dynamic of Ritual*. Leiden: Brill.

— (2007), 'Ritual dynamics and ritual failure', in U. Hüsken (ed.), *When Rituals Go Wrong: Mistakes, Failures, and the Dynamics of Ritual*. Leiden and Boston: Brill, pp. 337–66.

Hutchinson, Sharon E. (1996), *Nuer Dilemmas. Coping with Money, War, and the State*. Berkeley: University of California Press.

Hviding, Edvard (1996), 'Nature, culture, magic, science: on meta-languages for comparison in cultural ecology', in P. Descola and G. Pálsson (eds), *Nature and Society: Anthropological Perspectives*. London and New York: Routledge, pp. 165–84.

Ingold, Tim (1996), 'The optimal forager and economic man', in P. Descola and G. Pálsson (eds), *Nature and Society. Anthropological Perspectives*. London and New York: Routledge, pp. 25–44.

— (2011), *Being Alive. Essays on Movement, Knowledge and Description*. London and New York: Routledge.

Ingold, Tim and Jo Lee Vergunst, eds (2008), *Ways of Walking: Ethnography and Practice on Foot*. Aldershot, UK: Ashgate.

Innis, Robert E. (2005), 'The tacit logic of ritual embodiments: Rappaport and Polanyi between thick and thin', in D. Handelman and G. Lindquist (eds), *Ritual in Its Own Right*. New York and Oxford: Berghahn Books, pp. 197–212.

Irvine, Judith (2001), 'Formality and informality in communicative events', in A. Duranti (ed.), *Linguistic Anthropology*. Oxford: Blackwell Publishing, pp. 189–207.

Jackson, Michael, ed. (1996). *Things as They Are: New Directions in Phenomenological Anthropology*. Bloomington and Indianapolis: Indiana University Press.

Janowitz, Naomi (2011), 'Inventing the scapegoat: theories of sacrifice and ritual'. *Journal of Ritual Studies* 25, (1), 15–24.

Jarvie, Ian C. (1964), *The Revolution in Anthropology*. London: Routledge and Kegan Paul.

Johnstone, William, ed. (1995), *William Robertson Smith: Essays in Reassessment*. Sheffield, UK: Sheffield Academic Press.

Journal of Ritual Studies (2012), 'Special Issue, Ritual Framing: Gregory Bateson', with papers by Michael Houseman, Steven Engler and Mark Q. Gardiner, Eddy Plasquy, Jens Kreinath and Don Handelman. Comment by Andrew Strathern and Pamela J. Stewart (Strathern) (eds), 26, (2).

Juillerat, Bernard, ed. (1992), *Shooting the Sun: Ritual and Meaning in West Sepik*. Washington, DC: Smithsonian Institution Press.

Kapferer, Bruce (2004), 'Ritual dynamics and virtual practices: beyond representation and meaning', in D. Handelman and G. Lindquist (eds), *Ritual in its Own Right*. New York: Berghahn Books, pp. 35–54.

Kendall, Laurel (2006), 'When the shaman becomes a cultural icon, what happens to efficacy? Some observations from Korea', in K.-P. Köpping, B. Leistle and M. Rudolph (eds), *Ritual and Identity: Performative Practices as Effective Transformations of Social Reality*. Berlin: Lit Verlag, pp. 195–218.

Kitts, Margo (1999) Killing, Healing, and the Hidden Motif of Oath-Sacrifice in Iliad 21. *Journal of Ritual Studies* 13, (2), 42–57.

Köpping, Klaus-Peter, Bernhard Leistle and Michael Rudolph, eds (2006), *Ritual and Identity: Performative Practices as Effective Transformations of Social Reality*. Berlin: Lit Verlag.

Knottnerus, J. David (2011), *Ritual as a Missing Link: Sociology, Structural Ritualization Theory and Research*. Boulder and London: Paradigm Publishers.

Kreinath, Jens (2012a), 'Discursive formation, ethnographic encounter, photographic evidence: the centenary of Durkheim's basic forms of religious life and the anthropological study of Australian aboriginal religion in his time'. *Visual Anthropology* 25, (5), 367–420

— ed. (2012b), *The Anthropology of Islam Reader*. New York: Routledge.

Kreinath, Jens, Constance Hartung and Annette Deschner, eds (2004), *The Dynamics of Changing Rituals: The Transformation of Religious Rituals within Their Social and Cultural Context*. Toronto Studies in Religion Vol. 29. Donald Wiebe, (Gen ed.), New York, Washington, DC/Baltimore, Bern, Frankfurt am Main, Berlin, Brussels, Vienna and Oxford: Peter Lang.

Kreinath, Jens, Jan Snoek and Michael Stausberg, eds (2006a), 'Ritual studies, ritual theory, theorizing rituals – an introductory essay', in J. Kreinath, J. Snoek and M. Stausberg (eds), *Theorizing Rituals: Issues, Topics, Approaches, Concepts*. Leiden and Boston: Brill, pp. xiii–xxv.

— (2006b), *Theorizing Rituals: Issues,Topics, Approaches, Concepts*. Leiden and Boston: Brill.

Kuehling, Susanne (2005), *Dobu: Ethics of Exchange on a Massim Island, Papua New Guinea*. Honolulu: University of Hawai'i Press.

Kuper, Adam, ed. (1977), *The Social Anthropology of Radcliffe-Brown*. London: Routledge and Kegan Paul.

Laidlaw, James (2004), 'Introduction', in H. Whitehouse and J. Laidlaw (eds), *Ritual and Memory*. Walnut Creek: Alta Mira Press, pp. 1–10.

— (2007), 'A well-disposed social anthropologist's problems with the "Cognitive Science" of Religion', in, H. Whitehouse and J. Laidlaw (eds), *Religion, Anthropology and Cognitive Science*. Durham, NC: Carolina Academic Press, pp. 211–46.

Lane, Jeremy F. (2000), *Pierre Bourdieu. A Critical Introduction*. London: Pluto Press.

Latour, Bruno (2010), *On the Modern Cult of the Factish Gods*. Durham, NC: Duke University Press.

Lawrence, Peter (1964), *Road Belong Cargo*. Manchester: Manchester University Press.

Lawson, E. T. and R. N. McCauley (1990), *Rethinking Religion: Connecting Cognition and Culture*. Cambridge: Cambridge University Press.

Lazer, Estelle (2010), *Resurrecting Pompeii*. London and New York: Routledge.

Leach, Edmund Ronald (1954), *Political Systems of Highland Burma: A Study of Kachin Social Structure*. London: The Athlone Press.

Leistle, Bernhard (2006), 'Ritual as sensory communication: a theoretical and analytical perspective', in K.-P. Köpping, B. Leistle and M. Rudolph (eds), *Ritual and Identity: Performative Practices as Effective Transformations of Social Reality*. Berlin: Lit Verlag, pp. 33–73.

Lévi-Strauss, Claude (1963), *Structural Anthropology*. New York: Basic Books.

— (1966), *The Savage Mind* (translation of *La Pensée Sauvage* 1962). Chicago: The University of Chicago Press.

— (1969), *The Elementary Structures of Kinship*. Boston: Beacon Press.

— (1978), *Myth and Meaning*. London: Routledge and Kegan Paul.

Lévy-Bruhl, Lucien (1910), *Les Fonctions Mentales dans les Sociétés Inférieures*. Paris: Félix Alcan.

— (1926), *How Natives Think*, Lilian A. Clare (trans.). London: George Allen and Unwin, Ltd. (Translation of: *Les Fonctions Mentales dans les Sociétés Inférieures*, Paris: Félix Alcan, 1922).

Lewis, Gilbert (2004), 'Religious doctrine or experience: a matter of seeing, learning, or doing', in H. Whitehouse and J. Laidlaw (eds), *Ritual and Memory: Toward a Comparative Anthropology of Religion*. Walnut Creek, Lanham, New York, Toronto, Oxford: Altamira Press, pp. 155–72.

Lienhardt, Godfrey (1961), *Divinity and Experience: The Religion of the Dinka*. Oxford: Clarendon Press.

Lindquist, Galina (2005), 'Bringing the soul back to the self: soul retrieval in neo-shamanism', in D. Handelman and G. Lindquist (eds), *Ritual in Its Own Right*. New York and Oxford: Berghahn Books, pp. 157–73.

LiPuma, Edward, Moishe Postone and Craig J Calhoun (1993), *Bourdieu: Critical Perspectives*. Chicago: University of Chicago Press.

Lock, Margaret and Nancy Scheper-Hughes (1987), 'The mindful body'. *Medical Anthropology Quarterly* 1, (1), 6–41.

Lorenz, Konrad (1966), *Evolution and modification of Behavior.* London: Methuen.

Lüddeckens, Dorothea (2006), 'Emotion', in J. Kreinath, J. Snoek and M. Stausberg (eds), *Theorizing Rituals: Issues, Topics, Approaches, Concepts.* Leiden and Boston: Brill, pp. 545–70.

Lüdtke, Karen (2009), *Dances with Spiders: Crisis, Celebrity and Celebration in Southern Italy.* Epistemologies of Healing Series, Vol. 4. New York and Oxford: Berghahn Books.

Lund, Katrín (2008), 'Listen to the sound of time: walking with Saints in an Andalusian village', in T. Ingold and J. L. Vergunst (eds), *Ways of Walking: Ethnography and Practice on Foot.* Aldershot: Ashgate, pp. 81–92.

Maine, Henry Sumner (1861) [1963], *Ancient Law: Its Connection with the Early History of Society and Its Relation to Modern Ideas.* Boston: Beacon Press.

Magowan, Fiona (2007), *Melodies of Mourning: Music and Emotion in Northern Australia.* Oxford: James Currey.

Malinowski, Bronislaw (1922), *Argonauts of the Western Pacific.* London: Routledge and Kegan Paul (published also by E.P. Dutton and Co., Inc., 1950).

— (1935), *Coral Gardens and Their Magic.* London: George Allen and Unwin.

— (1948), *Magic, Science, and Religion, and Other Essays.* Selected by Robert Redfield. Glencoe, IL: The Free Press.

Marett, Robert Ranulph (1914). *The Threshold of Religion* (2nd edn). New York: The Macmillan Company.

Mauss, Marcel (1990), *The Gift. The Form and Reason for Exchange in Archaic Societies*, W. D. Hall (trans.). London: Routledge (originally published 1923).

McClymond, Kathryn (2008), *Beyond Sacred Violence: A Comparative Study of Sacrifice.* Baltimore: The Johns Hopkins University Press.

McCorkle, Jr., William W. (2010), *Ritualizing the Disposal of the Deceased: From Corpse to Concept.* Toronto Studies in Religion Vol. 30, Donald Wiebe (Gen ed.). New York, Washington, DC/Baltimore, Bern, Frankfurt, Berlin, Brussels, Vienna, Oxford: Peter Lang.

Michaels, Axel (2006), 'Ritual and meaning', in J. Kreinath, J. Snoek and M. Stausberg (eds), *Theorizing Rituals: Issues, Topics, Approaches, Concepts.* Leiden and Boston: Brill, pp. 247–61.

Michaels, Axel, Anand Mishra, Lucia Dolce, Gil Raz and Katja Triplett, eds (2010), *Grammars and Morphologies of Ritual Practices in Asia. Ritual Dynamics and the Science of Ritual, Volume 1*, A. Michaels (Gen ed). Wiesbaden: Harrassowitz Verlag.

Moore, Jerry D. (2012), *Visions of Culture: An Introduction to Anthropological Theories and Theorists* (4th edn). Lanham, MD: AltaMira Press (a Division of Rowman & Littlefield).

Moore, Henrietta L. and Todd Sanders, eds (2006), *Anthropology in Theory: Issues in Epistemology.* Oxford, UK: Blackwell Publishing.

Moore, Sally Falk and Barbara G. Myerhoff, eds (1977), *Secular Ritual.* Amsterdam: Van Gorcum.

Morris, Rosalind C. (2006), 'Gender', in J. Kreinath, J. Snoek and M. Stausberg (eds), *Theorizing Rituals: Issues, Topics, Approaches, Concepts.* Leiden and Boston: Brill, pp. 361–78.

Murray, Gilbert (1927), 'Excursus on the ritual forms preserved in tragedy', in J. E. Harrison, *Themis: A Study of the Social Origins of Greek Religion* (2nd edn). Cambridge: Cambridge University Press, pp. 341–63.

Nelson, Christopher (2008), *Dancing with the Dead: Memory, Performance, and Everyday Life in Postwar Okinawa.* Durham and London: Duke University Press.

Palmer, Craig T., Lyle B. Steadman and Chris Cassidy (2006), 'Traditional religious ritual sacrifice: cultural materialism, costly signaling, or descendant-leaving strategy?' *Journal of Ritual Studies* 20, (2), 33–42.

Pedersen, Lene (2006), *Ritual and World Change in a Balinese Princedom.* Durham, NC: Carolina Academic Press.

Pemberton, John III, ed. (2000), *Insight and Artistry in African Divination.* Washington: Smithsonian Institution Press.

Philsooph, Hushang (1995), 'A reconsideration of Frazer's relationship with Robertson Smith: the myth and the facts', in William Johnstone (ed.), *William Robertson Smith: Essays in Reassessment.* Sheffield, UK: Sheffield Academic Press, pp. 331–42.

Pickering, W. S. F., ed. (2003, 2008), *Marcel Mauss on Prayer,* Susan Leslie (trans.). New York and Oxford: Durkheim Press/Berghahn Books.

Platvoet, Jan G. (2004), 'Ritual as war: on the need to de-Westernize the concept', in J. Kreinath, C. Hartung and A. Deschner (eds), *The Dynamics of Changing Rituals: The Transformation of Religious Rituals within Their Social and Cultural Context.* Toronto Studies in Religion Vol. 29. New York, Washington, DC/Baltimore, Bern, Frankfurt am Main, Berlin, Brussels, Vienna and Oxford: Peter Lang, pp. 243–66.

Pollock, Donald (2005), 'Masks and the semiotics of identity'. *JRAI* (N.S.), 1, 581–97.

Pouwer, Jan (2010), *Gender, Ritual and Social Formation: A Configurational Analysis Comparing Kamoro and Asmat.* Leiden: KITLV Press.

Quack, Johannes (2010) 'Bell, Bourdieu, and Wittgenstein on Ritual Sense', in W. Sax, J. Quack and J. Weinhold (eds), *The Problem of Ritual Efficacy*. Oxford: Oxford University Press, pp. 169–88.

Quack, Johannes and William S. Sax (2010), 'Introduction: The efficacy of rituals'. *Journal of Ritual Studies*, Special Issue on the efficacy of rituals 24, (1), 5–12.

Quack, Johannes and Paul Töbelmann (2010), 'Questioning "ritual efficacy"'. *Journal of Ritual Studies* 24, (1), 13–28.

Radcliffe-Brown and Alfred Reginald (1964), *The Andaman Islanders*. New York: The Free Press of Glencoe (originally published 1922 by Cambridge University Press).

— (1965), *Structure and Function in Primitive Society*. New York: The Free Press (first published 1952).

Ramos, Gabriela (2010), *Death and Conversion in the Andes: Lima and Cuzco, 1532–1670*. Notre Dame, IN: University of Notre Dame Press.

Rappaport, Roy A. (1968), *Pigs for the Ancestors: Ritual in the Ecology of a New Guinea People*. New Haven: Yale University Press.

— (1999), *Ritual and Religion in the Making of Humanity*. Cambridge: Cambridge University Press.

Rey, Terry (2007), *Bourdieu on Religion*. London: Equinox.

Riches, David (1986), 'The phenomenon of violence', in D. Riches (ed.), *The Anthropology of Violence*. Oxford: Basil Blackwell, pp. 1–27.

Roseman, Marina (1991), *Healing Sounds from the Malaysian Rainforest: Temiar Music and Medicine*. Berkeley, CA: University of California Press.

Rostas, Susanna (1998), 'From ritualization to performativity: the Concheros of Mexico', in Felicia Hughes-Freeland (ed.), *Ritual Performance, Media*. London and New York: Routledge, pp. 85–103.

Rudolph, Michael (2006), 'Competition among elites, ritual modification, and identity formation: the efficacy of the contemporary "Harvest-Festivals" of Taiwan's Ami', in K.-P. Köpping, B. Leistle and M. Rudolph (eds), *Ritual and Identity: Performative Practices as Effective Transformations of Social Reality*. Berlin: Lit Verlag, pp. 219–47.

— (2007), 'Failure of ritual reinvention? Efficacious new rituals among Taiwan's aborigines under the impact of religious conversion and competition between elites', in Ute Hüsken (ed.), *When Rituals Go Wrong: Mistakes, Failures, and the Dynamics of Ritual*. Leiden and Boston: Brill, pp. 325–36.

— (2008), 'Improvisation, contingency, and ambiguity: the efficacy of contemporary ritual performances of Taiwan's aborigines', in A. Henn and K.-P. Koepping (eds), *Rituals in an Unstable World: Contingency, Hybridity, Embodiment*. Frankfurt, Berlin, Bern, Bruxelles, New York and Wien: Peter Lang.

Samuel, Geoffrey (2010), 'Healing, efficacy, and the spirits'. *Journal of Ritual Studies* 24, (2), 7–20.

Sax, William S. (2009), *God of Justice: Ritual Healing and Social Justice in the Central Himalayas*. Oxford and New York: Oxford University Press.

Sax, William S., Johannes Quack and Jan Weinhold, eds (2010), *The Problem of Ritual Efficacy*. Oxford and New York: Oxford University Press.

Schechner, Richard (1985), *Between Theater and Anthropology. Intercultural Studies of Theater and Ritual*. Philadelphia: University of Pennsylvania Press.

Schieffelin, Edward L. (1996), 'On failure and performance. Throwing the medium out of the séance', in C. Laderman and M. Roseman (eds), *The Performance of Healing*. New York and London: Routledge, pp. 59–89.

— (2005). 'Problematizing performance', in Graham Harvey (ed.), *Ritual and Religious Belief: A Reader*. London and New York: Routledge, pp. 123–38.

— (2007), 'Introduction', in Ute Hüsken (ed.), *When Rituals Go Wrong: Mistakes, Failures, and the Dynamics of Ritual*. Leiden and Boston: Brill, pp. 1–20.

Schilbrack, Kevin (2004), 'Introduction: on the use of philosophy in the study of rituals', in K. Schilbrack (ed.), *Thinking through Rituals: Philosophical Perspectives*. New York and London: Routledge, pp. 1–30.

Scott, Michael W. (2007), *The Severed Snake. Matrilineages, Making Place, and a Melanesian Christianity in Southeast Solomon Islands*. Durham, NC: Carolina Academic Press.

Segal, Robert A. (1995), 'Smith versus Frazer on the comparative method', in W. Johnstone (ed.), *William Robertson Smith: Essays in Reassessment*. Sheffield, UK: Sheffield Academic Press, pp. 343–51.

— (2006), 'Myth and ritual', in J. Kreinath, J. Snoek and M. Stausberg (eds), *Theorizing Rituals: Issues, Topics, Approaches, Concepts*. Leiden and Boston: Brill, pp. 101–21.

Seligman, Adam B., Robert P. Weller, Michael J. Puett and Bennett Simon (2008), *Ritual and its Consequences: An Essay on the Limits of Sincerity*. New York: Oxford University Press.

Senft, Gunter and Ellen B. Basso, eds (2009), *Ritual Communication*. Oxford and New York: Berg.

Shipton, Parker (2007), *The Nature of Entrustment: Intimacy, Exchange, and the Sacred in Africa*. New Haven and London: Yale University Press.

Shulevitz, Judith (2010), *The Sabbath World: Glimpses of a Different Order of Time*. New York: Random House.

Simmel, Georg (1991), *Sociétés Secrètes*. Strasbourg: Circé.

Skafte, Dianne (1997), *Listening to the Oracle: The Ancient Art of Finding Guidance in the Signs and Symbols All Around Us*. San Francisco: HarperSanFrancisco, A Division of Harper Collins Publishers.

Skorupski, John (1976), *Symbol and Theory: A Philosophical Study of Theories of Religion in Social Anthropology*. Cambridge, London, New York and Melbourne: Cambridge University Press.

Smith, Catherine Cook (1930), *In Defense of Magic: The Meaning and Use of Symbol and Rite*. New York: Lincoln MacVeagh The Dial Press.

Smith, Jonathan Z. (1987), *To Take Place: Toward Theory in Ritual*. Chicago: The University of Chicago Press.

Smith, William Robertson (1969), *Lectures on the Religion of the Semites. The Fundamental Institutions*. New York: KTAV Publishing House (originally published by A. & C. Black in a revised ed., London 1894).

Sørensen, Jørgen Podemann (2006), 'Efficacy', in J. Kreinath, J. Snoek and M. Stausberg (eds), *Theorizing Rituals: Issues, Topics, Approaches, Concepts*. Leiden and Boston: Brill, pp. 523–31.

Sperber, Dan (1985), *On Anthropological Knowledge*. Cambridge: Cambridge University Press.

Stansbury-O'Donnell, Mark D. (2011), *Looking at Greek Art*. Cambridge: Cambridge University Press.

Steiner, Franz Baermann (1956a) [1999], 'Frazer and his critic Marett', in Jeremy Adler and Richard Fardon (eds), *Franz Baermann Steiner: Selected Writings. Vol. 1: Taboo, Truth, and Religion*. New York and Oxford: Berghahn Books, pp. 171–80.

— (1956b) [1999], 'Van Gennep and Radcliffe-Brown', in Jeremy Adler and Richard Fardon (eds), *Franz Baermann Steiner: Selected Writings. Vol. 1: Taboo, Truth, and Religion*. New York and Oxford: Berghahn Books, pp. 189–96.

— (1956c) [1999], 'A Victorian problem: Robertson Smith', in Jeremy Adler and Richard Fardon (eds), *Franz Baermann Steiner: Selected Writings. Vol. 1: Taboo, Truth, and Religion*. New York and Oxford: Berghahn Books, pp. 132–9.

Stewart, Pamela J. and Andrew J. Strathern (1999), 'Female spirit cults as a window on gender relations in the highlands of Papua New Guinea', *The Journal of the Royal Anthropological Institute* 5, (3): 345–60.

— eds (2000), *Identity Work: Constructing Pacific Lives*. ASAO (Association for Social Anthropology in Oceania) Monograph Series No. 18. Pittsburgh: University of Pittsburgh Press.

— (2001), *Humors and Substances: Ideas of the Body in New Guinea.* Westport, Conn. and London: Bergin and Garvey, Greenwood Publishing Group.

— (2002a), *Gender, Song, and Sensibility: Folktales and Folksongs in the Highlands of New Guinea.* Westport, CT: Praeger.

— (2002b), *Remaking the World: Myth, Mining and Ritual Change among the Duna of Papua New Guinea.* Washington, DC: Smithsonian Institution Press.

— (2002c), *Violence: Theory and Ethnography.* London and New York: Continuum.

— (2003), *Landscape, Memory, and History: Anthropological Perspectives.* London: Pluto Press.

— (2004), *Witchcraft, Sorcery, Rumors and Gossip.* Cambridge, UK: Cambridge University Press.

— eds (2005), *Contesting Rituals: Islam and Practices of Identity-Making.* Durham, NC: Carolina Academic Press

— (2007), 'Introduction: ritual practices, "cultural revival" movements, and historical change', in Stewart, Pamela J. and Andrew Strathern (eds), *Asian Ritual Systems.* Durham, NC: Carolina Academic Press, pp. 3–33.

— eds (2008), *Exchange and Sacrifice.* For, Ritual Studies Monograph Series, Durham, NC: Carolina Academic Press.

— (2009), 'Growth of the Mazu complex in Cross-Straits contexts (Taiwan and Fujian Province, China)'. *Journal of Ritual Studies* 23, (1), 67–72.

— eds (2010), *Ritual.* Farnham, UK: Ashgate Publishing.

Stewart, Pamela J. and Andrew J. Strathern and Jürgen Trantow (2011), *Melpa-German-English Dictionary.* Pittsburgh: University of Pittsburgh Library System.

Strathern, Andrew J. (1971), *The Rope of Moka: Big-men and ceremonial exchange in Mount Hagen, New Guinea.* Cambridge, UK: Cambridge University Press.

— (1973), 'Kinship, descent, and locality: some New Guinea examples', in Jack Goody (ed.), *The Character of Kinship.* Cambridge: Cambridge University Press, pp. 21–34.

— (1992), 'Exegesis, comparison, and interpretation', in B. Juillerat (ed.), *Shooting the Sun.* Washington, DC: Smithsonian Institution Press, pp. 260–7.

— (1996), *Body Thoughts.* Ann Arbor, MI: University of Michigan Press.

— (2007) [Re-issued with new Preface by A. Strathern and P.J. Stewart], *The Rope of Moka.* Cambridge, UK: Cambridge University Press.

— (2009) [1982], *Inequality in New Guinea Highlands Society.* Cambridge, UK: Cambridge University Press.

Strathern, Andrew and Pamela J. Stewart (1997), 'The efficacy-entertainment braid revisited: from ritual to commerce in Papua New Guinea'. *Journal of Ritual Studies* 11, (1), 61–70.

— (1998), 'Embodiment and communication: two frames for the analysis of ritual'. *Social Anthropology* 6, (2), 237–51.

— (1999a), *'The Spirit is Coming!' A Photographic-Textual Exposition of the Female Spirit Cult Performance in Mount Hagen*. Pittsburgh: Deixis Foundation.

— (1999b), 'Outside and inside meanings: Non-verbal modalities of agonistic communication among the Wiru of Papua New Guinea'. *Man and Culture in Oceania* 15, 1–22.

— (2000), *Arrow Talk: Transaction, Transition, and Contradiction in New Guinea Highlands History*. Kent, Ohio and London: Kent State University Press.

— (2001), 'Rappaport's Maring: the challenge of ethnology', in Ellen Messner and Michael Lambek (eds), *Ecology and the Sacred: Engaging the Anthropology of Roy Rappaport*. Ann Arbor: The University of Michigan Press.

— (2004), *Empowering the Past, Confronting the Future: The Duna People of Papua New Guinea*. New York: Palgrave Macmillan.

— (2008a), 'Introduction: aligning words, aligning worlds', in P. J. Stewart and A. Strathern (eds), *Exchange and Sacrifice*. Durham, NC: Carolina Academic Press, pp. xi–xxxvi.

— (2008b), 'Exchange and sacrifice: examples from Papua New Guinea', in P. J. Stewart and A. Strathern (eds), *Exchange and Sacrifice*. Durham, NC: Carolina Academic Press, pp. 229–45.

— (2008c), 'Shamanic performances: issues of performativity and comparison'. *Journal of Ritual Studies* 22, (1), 53–66.

— (2008d), 'Embodiment theory in performance and performativity'. *Journal of Ritual Studies* 22, (1), 67–72.

— (2009), 'Introduction: a complexity of contexts, a multiplicity of changes', in P. J. Stewart and A. Strathern (eds), *Religious and Ritual Change: Cosmologies and Histories*. Durham, NC: Carolina Academic Press, pp. 3–68.

— (2010a), 'Kinship, ritual, cosmos'. *Journal de la Société des Océanistes*, 130–1, 79–88.

— (2010b), 'Comment: functions, effects, and efficacy: a moving walkway of analysis'. *Journal of Ritual Studies* 24, (1), 1–4.

— (2010c), 'Comment: Part II, functions, effects, and efficacy: further considerations on a moving walkway of analysis'. *Journal of Ritual Studies* 24, (2), 1–6.

— (2010d), 'Embodiment and communication: two frames for the analysis of ritual', in P. J. Stewart and A. Strathern (eds), *Ritual*. Farnham, UK: Ashgate Publishing, pp. 83–97.

— (2011), 'Embodiment and personhood', in Frances E. Mascia-Lees (ed.), *A Companion to the Anthropology of the Body and Embodiment*. Oxford, UK: Wiley-Blackwell Ltd, pp. 388–402.

Stroeken, Koen (2004), 'In search of the real: the healing contingency of Sukuma divination', in M. Winkelman and P. M. Peek (eds), *Divination and Healing*. Tucson: The University of Arizona Press, pp. 29–54.

Sutton, Donald S. (2003), *Steps of Perfection. Exorcistic Performers and Chinese Religion in Twentieth Century Taiwan*. Cambridge, MA and London: Harvard University Asia Center.

Szonyi, Michael (2007), 'The virgin and the Chinese state: the cult of Wang Yulan and the politics of local identity in Jinmen (Quemoy)', in Pamela J. Stewart and Andrew Strathern (eds), *Asian Ritual Systems: Syncretisms and Ruptures*. Durham, NC: Carolina Academic Press.

Tambiah, Stanley J. (1968), 'The magical power of words'. *Man*, (n.s.), 3, 185–206.

— (1990), *Magic, Science, Religion, and the Scope of Rationality*. Cambridge, UK: Cambridge University Press.

Throop, C. Jason and Charles D. Laughlin (2002), 'Ritual, collective effervescence, and the categories: toward a neo-Durkheimian model of the nature of human consciousness, feeling, and understanding'. *Journal of Ritual Studies* 16, (1), 40–63.

Toner, Jerry (2010), *Popular Culture in Ancient Rome*. Cambridge: Polity Press.

Tremlin, Todd (2006), *Minds and Gods. The Cognitive Foundations of Religion*. Oxford: Oxford University Press.

Trulsson, Åsa (2010), *Cultivating the Sacred: Ritual Creativity and Practice among Women in Contemporary Europe*. Lund Studies in History of Religions, Vol. 28. Tord Olsson (Gen ed.). Lund, Sweden: Lund University.

Turner, Edith (2004), 'Drumming, divination, and healing: the community at work', in M. Winkelman and P. M. Peek (eds), *Divination and Healing*. Tucson: University of Arizona Press, pp. 55–80.

— (2012), *Communitas: The Anthropology of Collective Joy*. New York: Palgrave Macmillan.

Turner, Edith with William Blodgett, Singleton Kahona and Fideli Benwa (1992), *Experiencing Ritual: A New Interpretation of African Healing*. Philadelphia: University of Pennsylvania Press.

Turner, Terence (2008), 'Ritualized politics and politicized ritual among ourselves and the Kayapo of Brazil', in A. Henn and K.-P. Koepping (eds), *Rituals in an Unstable World: Contingency, Hybridity,*

Embodiment. Frankfurt, Berlin, Bern, Bruxelles, New York and Wien: Peter Lang, pp. 133–47.

Turner, Victor (1967), *The Forest of Symbols: Aspects of Ndembu Ritual*. Ithaca, NY: Cornell University Press.

— (1968), *The Drums of Affliction. A Study of the Religious Processes among the Ndembu of Zambia*. Oxford: Clarendon Press and The International African Institute.

— (1969), *The Ritual Process: Structure and Anti-Structure*. New York: Cornell University Press.

— (1982), *From Ritual to Theatre: The Human Seriousness of Play*. New York: PAJ Publications.

— (1985a), 'The anthropology of performance', in E. Turner (ed.), *On the Edge of the Bush*. Tucson: University of Arizona Press, pp. 177–204

— (1985b), *On the Edge of the Bush. Anthropology as Experience*. Collected essays of Victor Turner. Edith L. B. Turner (ed.), Tucson, Arizona: The University of Arizona Press..

— (1992), *Blazing the Trail: Way Marks in the Exploration of Symbols*. Collected essays of Victor Turner. Edith L. B. Turner (ed.). Tucson and London: The University of Arizona Press.

— (1996) [1957], *Schism and Continuity in an African Society*. Manchester: Manchester University Press.

Turner, Victor W. and Edward M. Bruner, eds (1986), *The Anthropology of Experience*. Urbana and Chicago: University of Illinois Press.

Tuzin, Donald (1992), 'Revelation and concealment in the cultural organization of meaning: a methodological note', in B. Juillerat (ed.), *Shooting the Sun*. Washington, DC: Smithsonian Institution Press, pp. 251–9.

Tylor, Sir Edward Burnett (1970), *Religion in Primitive Culture*. Introduction by Paul Radin. Gloucester, MA: Peter Smith, (reprint of *Primitive Culture*, 1958, vol. 2, originally published in 1871, London: John Murray).

Vásquez, Manuel A. (2011), *More than Belief: A Materialist Theory of Religion*. Oxford and New York: Oxford University Press.

Vernant, Jean-Pierre (2001), *The Universe, The Gods, and Men*. Linda Asher (trans.). New York: Harper Collins. (First published in French in 1999.)

Volkman, Toby Alice (1985), *Feasts of Honor: Ritual Change in the Toraja Highlands*. Illinois Studies in Anthropology No. 16. Urbana and Chicago: University of Chicago Press.

Wagner, Roy (1972), *Habu. The Innovation of Meaning in Daribi Religion*. Chicago: The University of Chicago Press.

— (1981), *The Invention of Culture*. Chicago: The University of Chicago Press.

Wang-Riese, Xiaobing and Thomas O. Höllmann, eds (2009), *Time and Ritual in Early China*. Wiesbaden: Harrassowitz Verlag.

Whitehouse, Harvey and James Laidlaw, eds (2004), *Ritual and Memory: Toward a Comparative Anthropology of Religion*. Walnut Creek, Lanham, New York, Toronto, Oxford: Altamira Press.

— eds (2007), *Religion, Anthropology, and Cognitive Science*. Durham, NC: Carolina Academic Press.

Wingo, Camille (2012), *Pictures Making Beliefs: A Cognitive Technological Model for Ritual Efficacy*. Durham, NC: Carolina Academic Press.

Winkelman, Michael and Philip M. Peek, eds (2004), *Divination and Healing. Potent Vision*. Tucson: The University of Arizona Press.

Wulf, Christoph (2006), 'Praxis', in J. Kreinath, J. Snoek and M. Stausberg (eds), *Theorizing Rituals: Issues, Topics, Approaches, Concepts*. Leiden and Boston: Brill, pp. 395–411.

Xygalatas, Dimitris (2012), *The Burning Saints. Cognition and Culture in the Fire-Walking Rituals of the Anastenaria*. Sheffield: Equinox Publishing.

Young, Michael W. (1971), *Fighting with Food. Leadership, Values, and Social Control in a Massim Society*. Cambridge, UK: Cambridge University Press.

Zotter, Astrid and Christof Zotter (2010), *Hindu and Buddhist Initiations in India and Nepal*. Ethno-Indology. Heidelberg Studies in South Asian Rituals, Volume 10. Axel Michaels (Gen ed.). Wiesbaden: Harrassowitz Verlag.

Index